Entrepreneurial

Transitions

Mike,

Enjoy Your Journey!

Roy F.

Entrepreneurial Transitions

From Entrepreneurial Genius to Visionary Leader

Roy F. Cammarano

Griffin Publishing
Glendale, California

10   9   8   7   6   5   4   3   2

ISBN 1-882180-15-1

Griffin Publishing
Glendale, California

Manufactured in the United States of America.

Foreword

The *Entrepreneurial Revolution* has changed forever the structure of Corporate America. We are traveling down economic highways whose courses have yet to be charted. Entrepreneurs are the driving forces that are piloting us, headlong into the unknown. Neither Government nor the business community understand Entrepreneurs. Even more disturbing, they don't understand themselves. In this book, Roy offers some inspiring answers to Entrepreneurs, as they travel down the lonely and terrorizing path from "start-up" to running a successful, fully staffed organization. This is one of those rare books that should be read then reread every six months, by every CEO running a "growing company."

In my book, *For Entrepreneurs Only*, I claim that the greatest single cause of entrepreneurial failure, is our inability to make the transition from "small" to "large"—to "let go." In Roy's words "to move from 'Entrepreneurial Genius' to 'Visionary Leader.'" The path to success is littered with the skeletons of individuals who failed that test.

I believe that "Freedom" is the motivational force behind every Entrepreneur. Free to get our head above the crowd; free to be our own person; free to have ideas, and make those ideas into companies; free to be free. Isn't it amazing that we Entrepreneurs, who risk everything for that incredible feeling, are the same ones who would deny it to the people we employ; and in so doing fail to make the "Entrepreneurial Transition."

I wish you good reading,

Wilson L. Harrell
Entrepreneur of the Year 1991
Special Contributor, *Success Magazine*
Former Publisher, *Inc. Magazine*

Dedication

To my parents,
Frank and Evelyn,
whose love and support encouraged
me to take risks, accept challenges and realize dreams.

Aloha

Contents

ACKNOWLEDGMENTS

I would like to acknowledge all of the entrepreneurs who are today just beginning to dream their dreams and those who are already realizing their dreams and creating a better tomorrow.

I would also like to thank the many special people who have shared their gifts with me, taught me new ways of thinking, feeling and seeing.

The "reality" of this book is in itself a testament to a multitude of people, all of them friends, some, clients as well.

Thank you to my wife Mary Jo for incredible patience throughout this difficult process and to my clients who contributed so much and who graciously allowed me to share some of their successes as well as their "learning experiences."

This book would not have been possible without the words and wisdom of Marjean Daniels. Her friendship, guidance and assistance have been invaluable and are greatly appreciated. Many others have helped by encouraging me, prodding me and by holding me to standards that I hope will help entrepreneurs attain a new level of excellence.

Introduction

We are shifting from a managerial society to an entrepreneurial society.

—John Naisbitt

At some point in their careers, many of the most charismatic and influential business people in this country have been or are entrepreneurs. Inspired geniuses, risk-takers and motivated visionaries, they are apt to be on the cutting edge of their industries, blazing the trail and experiencing unprecedented successes.

We still hold entrepreneurial geniuses like Andrew Carnegie, Henry Ford, John D. Rockefeller, Ted Turner, Tom Watson, Sr., Debbie Fields, H. Ross Perot, John Sculley, Bill Gates and Mary Kay Ash in high esteem for having realized the "great American dream."

Yet a baffling phenomenon that can stifle growth often occurs in these entrepreneurial genius organizations. Inevitably, as the businesses prosper and expand, the founding geniuses discover they and their organizations are changing, and not always for the better. Instead of maturing along parallel lines, they seem to grow in opposite directions along the developmental curve. The organization advances at a different pace than does the entrepreneurial genius who started it all.

When companies experience this situation, the fun of creating an exciting new venture and the joy in sharing the successes and occasional failures soon disappears. A sense of discomfort and resentment permeate the company. Before too long, entrepreneurs become painfully aware that they are no longer in control of their own businesses.

What happens? Is the answer to this phenomenon simply that organizational growth has surpassed the entrepreneur's capacity to manage it? Perhaps. Even though the company may be experiencing tremendous success, many entrepreneurs unwittingly create chaos because they have not acquired the appropriate management skills to guide and sustain an organization's long-term development.

Another factor that contributes to the confusion is entrepreneurial behavior—which tends to be erratic at best. As part and parcel of the entrepreneurial genius, this trait can be extremely limiting as organizations mature. What ensues almost always affects the corporate culture adversely.

When entrepreneurs appreciate how the dynamics of their behavior influence the future viability of the organization, they quickly grasp an understanding of *why* they need to make a behavioral transition and can become Visionary Leaders virtually overnight.

In an attempt to remedy problems in the company, most entrepreneurial geniuses believe the fault lies everywhere but with themselves. How could they be wrong when they literally birthed the business through their vision, courage, and risk-taking?

Unwilling or unable to pinpoint the specific source of the problems, however, entrepreneurial geniuses typically go through identifiable behavioral phases in an attempt to restore the organization to its original, pristine state. They try to use the same recipe even though the ingredients have changed. This results more often than not in a disaster.

Because they are leaders by their very nature, entrepreneurial geniuses believe if they just take care of employees and assume command of all problems, everything will return to "normal." Unfortunately, this tendency leads the entrepreneur to enter what I call the Benevolent Dictator phase.

Managing a growing and ever-changing organization is especially difficult for entrepreneurs because their personality traits and behaviors are often diametrically opposed to employee and organizational needs. Behaviorist Abraham Maslow believed that human beings share common inner needs. When individual higher needs are satisfied, a person can reach their full potential and become self-actualized as a peak performer. When inner needs are ignored, employees may manifest their "lack" by being unproductive or even uncooperative.

Entrepreneurial Geniuses are independent, self-reliant and usually self-actualized. Those who choose to work for others (employees) normally need assistance in becoming self-actualized. Many entrepreneurs are unaware of this distinction and therefore cannot address an effective solution. Hence, their first reaction is to become a Benevolent Dictator, making every decision based on their own perspective, wearing several "hats," and refusing to delegate to others. They keep a tight rein on every function in the organization in the hopes of controlling the outcomes.

However much Benevolent Dictators may be willing to delegate responsibility and accountability, they often refuse to assign the authority that accompanies those responsibilities and accountabilities. As a result, employees often become resentful to the point of sabotaging their positions and, at times, the very existence of the organization.

Because Benevolent Dictators think everything they need to know is in their own heads, there is little communication in these organizations. Poor communication inhibits cooperation and results in a complete absence of collaboration. Businesses in this mode can quickly grind to a halt.

Frustrated when they fail to successfully correct problems or address concerns, Benevolent Dictators may then decide to leave the management of the company up to employees. In this way, Benevolent Dictators default into being Disassociated Directors. However, as the description implies, this behavioral change increases the distance between the entrepreneur and the organization and fails to recapture "the dream."

Disassociated Directors may throw down the following challenge: "All right, you employees think you know so much about running an organization, see what you can do. Go ahead!"

But Disassociated Directors cannot truly hand over the reins of decision making because they do not trust anyone except themselves.

Even if they do allow a few decisions to be made by others, they always have a need to interfere with the implementation of the decision or, in some cases, will even countermand it. Thus employees, in turn, grow to distrust entrepreneurial behavior because it appears inconsistent and unpredictable.

Understanding entrepreneurial behaviors, appreciating the motivations behind those behaviors, and modifying them can help shift Entrepreneurial Geniuses, Benevolent Dictators and Disassociated Directors into Visionary Leaders.

Visionary Leaders build companies that communicate, cooperate and collaborate. They share Values, Vision and Mission with the organization and its customers. They create purpose-driven organizations that achieve goals, meet objectives and provide satisfaction for employees and customers.

Even though they share common characteristics, each entrepreneur is unique unto themselves and the challenges their entrepreneurial enterprises face are diverse. This book was written to assist entrepreneurs who desire to acquire the skills they personally need so they can apply those skills to their own specific businesses.

The information contained in these pages should also be useful to people who work for or with entrepreneurial enterprises in bettering their understanding of what is happening in the organization and why.

The tools, techniques, processes, strategies and concepts presented in this book have been developed over many years of working with entrepreneurs and their organizations. Proven application to a broad audience led me to the idea of capturing them in a format that allowed others to share and try out for themselves.

I have found that awareness is the key to making the shift from an Entrepreneurial Genius to a true Visionary Leader. In this book, the entrepreneur will explore:

- *how to lead and manage their organization into the next century*
- *how entrepreneurial behavior affects the corporate culture*
- *why gathering various perspectives is vital to survival*
- *why a change in entrepreneurial behavior is critical to the long-term viability of any business.*

Two major behavioral issues entrepreneurs have difficulty with as their organizations grow are decision making and delegation. A Decision Making Process Model debuts in this book that addresses the first area. It is simple to use and ensures that, in a timely fashion, readers can gather the information they need to arrive at the best possible decisions for the circumstances.

I also explain why delegation is so important to the success of the entrepreneurial organization and describe how entrepreneurs can assign authority, accountability and responsibility for work functions without delegating away their leadership role.

Readers will also learn to:

- *identify where they and their organizations are on the developmental curve*
- *recognize the different phases and stages of entrepreneurial growth*
- *gain a perspective on specifically which entrepreneurial behaviors affect the organization adversely*
- *reduce the pain of entrepreneurial transitions*
- *acquire the professional management skills of Visionary Leadership.*

Entrepreneurs can learn to modify behavior without sacrificing the wonderful freedom-loving spirit that characterizes these innovative, charismatic people. In the process, entrepreneurs can influence and empower others to be the best they can be. Rather than putting out fires, entrepreneurs can invest their time leading an organization focused on contributing to a better world for everyone.

It is my sincere hope you will derive value and benefit from reading this book. Realizing "the dream" is still a goal for most entrepreneurial-minded people. Given the number of entrepreneurial businesses that continue to crop up every year, I can safely assume the pursuit of the dream is still alive.

Roy F. Cammarano
Dana Point, California

Chapter 1

The Entrepreneurial Journey:
The Realities of Pursuing the Dream

What the mind of man can conceive and believe, the mind of a man can achieve.

—Napoleon Hill

Entrepreneurial Contributions

Charismatic and innovative risk-takers, entrepreneurs represent achievement and success to almost everyone they encounter. They intuitively seem to know what the public wants; their active minds create niches for products and services where none existed before.

Entrepreneurial contributions to business and the community are legendary. Few are admired more than those who have risen to the top of their industries such as H. Ross Perot of EDS and Perot Systems; Debbie Fields of Mrs. Fields Cookies; David Hewlett and William Packard of Hewlett-Packard; William H. Gates III of Microsoft; and Mary Kay Ash of Mary Kay Cosmetics.

Brilliant visionaries, entrepreneurs often begin companies with little more than a clever idea. Enthusiasm alone appears to transport them to dizzying heights of prosperity. Countless stories abound of business breakthroughs created by men and women who have succeeded as entrepreneurs because of an ardent belief in the need for and value of their product or service.

The entrepreneurs' passionate faith in their vision and a commitment to its realization often become tantamount to a religion. Intensely dedicated to their new business venture, entrepreneurs easily convert employees into instant believers.

If roadblocks and obstacles surface along the way, they are apt to be overcome just by the very nature of entrepreneurial zeal. In need of capital or credit, entrepreneurial energy tends to charm even the most inflexible banker. If the entrepreneur requires staff to work overtime filling orders that are flooding in, employees do so willingly.

With the world virtually at their feet, it is obvious why entrepreneurs believe this state of affairs will continue indefinitely.

Clouds on the Horizon

Yet, there inevitably comes a time in the growth of most entrepreneurial organizations when their founders discover they are running a company they don't recognize. The entrepreneur can't identify when or even how the organization changed.

The signs are subtle, and no one can point to any one cause for the general feeling of uneasiness. This shift in the corporate environment seems unwarranted with the company growing at a tremendous rate and experiencing what appears to be unprecedented success.

However, hairline cracks appear in the foundation: various departments are fighting among themselves; vendors aren't cooperating; and employees don't act as if they are interested in doing their jobs with anything resembling commitment and excellence.

There may be breakdowns in communication resulting in slowed sales or missed appointments. The shipping department may be totally overwhelmed with orders that back up due to someone failing to secure the raw materials necessary to fill those requests.

Other signs indicate further disorder. Invoicing becomes slipshod and sporadic. The overworked bookkeeper falls behind in collections. Cash flow dries up. The entrepreneur/founder always seems to be out on appointments, leaving the young company to run itself.

In spite of company growth, there is a distinct change in the atmosphere within the organization. After the first flush of success, and particularly with continuing expansion, the company appears to be deteriorating. Employees sense these hairline cracks are widening into deep chasms.

As staff members observe these breakdowns, they begin to doubt the entrepreneur's ability to manage and their own capacity to deal with problems. Whereas, initially, they trusted blindly in the company, their attitudes now reflect a general skepticism pervading the entire organization.

At this point, the excitement of creating and realizing "the dream" has vanished for both the entrepreneur and the employees. Much of the euphoria entrepreneurs feel in the beginning soon dissipates. They can no longer keep their attention focused on the tasks at hand. The dream is not "fun" anymore. Even as the company flourishes, it seems on the verge of self-destruction.

In the midst of this disarray, employees tend to develop a "foxhole" mentality and do only that which is necessary to maintain their positions. They're neither as open nor as willing to share with their employer as they once did. The sense of closeness is gone. Mistrust grows. It is evident some serious concerns must be addressed before too long.

What goes wrong? Do entrepreneurs peak? Is there a common malady that specifically afflicts entrepreneurial organizations? If so, is anyone in particular at fault or is this attributable to the natural cycle of growth and maturation?

Storm Warnings

This situation entrepreneurs find themselves in parallels that of new parents faced with the responsibility of raising their first child. During the initial stages of growth, caring for a baby is less complicated because the infant is confined, out of necessity, to the crib, playpen or high chair.

The baby is totally dependent on the parent, trusting it implicitly, just as the young entrepreneurial organization is dependent upon the founder. Controlling all of the variables, parents reign supreme.

As in the parent/child relationship, all the needs of the infant organization are being met by the parent/entrepreneur. However, as children grow, their needs change. A two-year old child requires different treatment than a newborn baby. The household must shift to accommodate the child's natural development.

The same holds true for a growing company. Organizations must adapt to changing needs at various stages of its growth and development. When the company is young and supported by a few staff members, the handling of various management responsibilities is comparatively easy.

However, as company growth demands additional employees and departments, acquiring more sophisticated management skills allows the entrepreneur to expand the company while capitalizing on its initial success. Reasons for a setback to the entrepreneurial dream and the subsequent disappointments that follow may include: miscommunication, poor planning, or ineffective management and decision making.

Problems center most often around a lack of communication. Organizations in distress or experiencing "growing pains" may discover, although the entrepreneurial owner has definite goals in mind, no one else in the company seems to understand clearly what these goals are. Perhaps entrepreneurs assume policies, procedures and systems have been instituted simply because they know what to do and believe everyone else should know too.

Many entrepreneurs, whose minds operate light years ahead of employee comprehension, have a tendency to believe that what is perfectly obvious to them is therefore understood by all. The entrepreneur may devise an innovative new marketing strategy to increase sales tenfold; however, unless the concept is shared with and understood by the employees, the likelihood of the strategy being fully implemented is slim.

At what point do employees lose their sense of community? Is the Peter Principle at work? Has the entrepreneur risen to a level of incompetence? Is the company managed to maintain the entrepreneur's individual self-worth, or to support the growth and development of all?

Efficiency versus Effectiveness

Entrepreneurs may experience other problems and concerns because they have not expended time and effort planning for contingencies, nor have they identified specific long-term outcomes they wish to achieve. They may have only a vague idea of company resources or the true state of corporate finances. Many have no idea where their own organizations stand regarding personnel training procedures or other vital company functions.

Even though they are efficient, many entrepreneurial organizations stop growing because they are not effective. Internationally recognized business consultant and author Peter Drucker notes:

Efficiency is doing things right.

Effectiveness is doing the right *things...*

Most managers are efficient but not all are effective. If a manager has twenty-five areas of responsibility but twelve do not specifically lead to results directly affecting the viability of the organization, the manager may be efficient but not effectively managing. Time spent on twelve non-essentials is really just wasted effort.

Efficiency is fairly easy to achieve; effectiveness is much more difficult. Some entrepreneurial organizations are marvelously efficient at doing the *wrong* things. They justify the situation by rationalizing: "This is how we've always done it here" or "It worked the last time we did it that way."

A company might deliver its product or service to customers on time, demonstrating efficiency, but at what cost? Are employees overworked in order to meet deadlines? If so, good employees eventually leave. Subsequently, the company must recruit, hire, train, and motivate new personnel. This is always a costly endeavor—both in time and resources—making the company, at least temporarily, ineffective.

Creating effective organizations means developing more effective people. By focusing on doing the *right* things and implementing systematic and proven approaches, employee effectiveness can improve dramatically.

People-Dependent Versus Person-Dependent Systems

Often an entrepreneur finds an employee who is skilled in a specific area and then develops systems around that employee. However, those systems are only effective as long as that person retains that position.

This is a natural process when organizations are young and a single individual often comprises an entire department. But, as the company expands, it requires systems that are people-dependent rather than person-dependent.

Perhaps a purchasing officer is skilled enough to create a computer program for tracking inventory. Unfortunately, they may be the only one who knows how to access or operate the program. Supposing the purchasing officer leaves the organization unexpectedly or is run over by a truck, no one else can then continue tracking inventory.

Person-dependent corporate structures result in an inherently-flawed design that cannot withstand the test of time. A system relying solely on one individual is limited in its growth at a later date. On the other hand, people-dependent systems are those set up so staff members are assigned to handle diverse tasks and trained to know and share systems.

Finding Calm in the Midst of Chaos

The most common cause of disenchantment in any entrepreneurial organization occurs when the company's growth

What does not occur to entrepreneurs in this circumstance is that their management style could be at fault or that they need to delegate instead of tenaciously holding the reins. Otherwise, management processes become major issues if entrepreneurs continue to be "all things to all people" and manage everything without assistance.

This "I am the parent" behavioral trait is shared by many entrepreneurs who insist on remaining in charge of every function of the company, believing they are the only ones who can do what needs to be done.

Balancing Behavior

Entrepreneurial organizations that flourish and grow are ones that successfully integrate the spirit of the entrepreneur with the functional capacity of the organization. The entrepreneur and the organization have developed a system permitting the entrepreneur to retain that independent entrepreneurial spirit while allowing the organization to be professionally managed in a more structured way.

An excellent example of this approach is Bill Gates, founder of Microsoft Corporation, a $7 billion computer software company headquartered in Redmond, Washington. After starting the business in 1975, Gates remains Chairman but has turned over the actual day-to-day control of operations to other executives. He serves as the Visionary Leader. All management decisions, although they encompass Gates' spirit and values, are made by professional managers.

He and his organization recruit the best talent available and then assign the appropriate authority, accountability, and responsibility the positions require. Gates has been quoted as saying:

I hire smart people and I challenge them to think.

There is a noticeable lack of bureaucracy within Microsoft, reflecting Gates' disdain for too many rules. Gates delegates heavily, allowing employees the freedom to make decisions;

however, he does acknowledge he is the greatest single influence on the corporate culture.

Most telling of Gates' visionary style of leadership is the environment he has created. It is based on the values he and his employees share, such as placing more importance on succeeding than on financial gain. Yet, the rewards are significant—more than 2,000 Microsoft employees have become millionaires.

Communication acts as a touchstone in the Microsoft organization. Sharing information is a high priority. Everyone is encouraged to believe they can make a difference, even change the world.

In contrast, consider the case of the celebrated computer genius who took his company to multi-million dollar success and was later thrown out by his own Board of Directors because, as the story goes, the founder's capricious actions and inconsistent decisions were endangering the future of the organization.

Refusing to delegate or relinquish control, Steven Jobs believed his entrepreneurial leadership style would make Apple Computer invincible. Jobs did indeed realize "his dream," but it was short-lived. He tried to run a global organization single-handedly instead of delegating to others. He was unable to make the shift from entrepreneur to Visionary Leader.

Today, having learned from his previous experience, Steven Jobs is now the respected CEO of NeXt Computers. He has now acquired the ability to delegate and brought in professional management much earlier in the process—an indication that Jobs appreciates the necessity to plan for long-term growth and corporate development.

Following the Path of Least Resistance

If entrepreneurs lack professional management skills and openly demonstrate a dislike for dealing with what they consider unnecessary, humdrum details of running a business—employee benefits, policies, performance reviews, formal reporting procedures—they will often succumb to their inclination to distance themselves from ever-increasing problems and unrest. Even making decisions becomes a nuisance and a bother.

As the company founders, they may believe they are the only people qualified to make decisions; yet, they quickly begin to feel overwhelmed when they have to deal with the myriad of details confronting them. Although most entrepreneurs are extremely adept at focusing on the conceptual side of their businesses, the signing of purchase orders and handling of trivia often get in the way of what they are willing and able to do. Their passion for creating new products and services and their vision of world success easily bog down in this day-to-day quagmire.

Unfortunately, entrepreneurs are not typically inclined to develop systems so others can handle these mundane matters. Consequently, because they feel a need to be in charge, entrepreneurs unknowingly aggravate the situation, perpetuating frustration and a feeling of disenchantment.

A growing company cannot afford to be run by a freewheeling non-conformist who finds uniformity irksome and bureaucracy detestable. Such a situation results in a company out of balance.

This imbalance, left unchecked during the heady, early stages of growth, is the main reason why a company may be forced to address these problems in later phases of development. During this stage, if the entrepreneur avoids making decisions and does not allow anyone else to take control, the business can grind to a halt.

According to Department of Commerce statistics, 50% of all small business start-ups in the United States are out of operation within the first year. Another 80% of the remaining 50% fall by the wayside by the end of the third year. For those remaining, the financial break-even point occurs at the end of the third year. As the odds of being successful are remote, anything an entrepreneur does to strengthen leadership abilities will eventually pay high dividends.

Calming Employee Rebellion

Without corporate structure, a company's future growth can be derailed. For any enterprise to experience sustained growth, it needs structure so employees know where and how they fit into the organization. Most employees prefer working under orderly conditions, trusting in management to be capable and competent, thus minimizing stress and confusion.

When tasks and duties are appropriately defined and assigned, through handbooks or training manuals, employees have documented evidence of organizational intent. If departments are not established, it is virtually impossible for employees to grow or seek advancement as no clear career paths exist for those who are ambitious.

Employee motivation to be productive increases when people are allowed to understand and develop trust in the organization. When purpose and policies are clarified, employees tend to respond positively, expressing more loyalty to a company addressing their needs and acknowledging their value rather than one that ignores their concerns.

Humans, by their very nature, want to know what is going on and need to be included as part of the corporate community. Inviting employees to participate in defining the importance of their specific activities to the overall efforts of the company enhances individual self-esteem, builds self-confidence, and creates *esprit de corps*.

Understanding management's goals and objectives and knowing how every member of the organization contributes to accomplishing those goals and objectives creates a workplace where employees mesh with each other and share a common view of success.

Some companies are like revolving doors and cannot keep personnel because they fail to recognize or accommodate employee inner needs. Even if salaries are high and jobs secure, most people have motivations other than financial. To many, the need to excel and take pride in their work is equally if not more important than compensation.

The deepest principle in human nature is the craving to be appreciated.

—William James

If employees believe their efforts are unappreciated, they will not see the value of their contribution to the company's products or services. Employees desire to be rewarded and recognized for talents and skills. If they are ignored or treated harshly, they become uncooperative and unproductive.

Establish Purpose Before Taking Action

Even though entrepreneurial passion can indeed carry the organization successfully along for a while, entrepreneurs will find it difficult to ultimately achieve goals and objectives without appropriate plans even if they are firmly focused on the future.

As entrepreneurs dislike formal systems and see them as restrictive, they resist the idea of having to be part of a bureaucratic organization and bound to follow guidelines. Some entrepreneurs understand they need to organize and delegate the many different accountabilities as the company grows. Yet, while they fully intend to establish and implement formal systems and structures, they are often so busy running the day-to-day operations they never seem to have quite enough time to do so.

In addition to being unwilling to spend the time, entrepreneurs have difficulty formally articulating and communicating their visions and goals or developing and writing a strategic plan. They feel it is unnecessary to invest valuable time transferring the plan in their heads to paper.

This attitude eventually causes the workforce to become apprehensive and anxious. A lack of formal planning results in management by "crisis to crisis"—a challenge entrepreneurs welcome as they thrive on chaos. However, continual crisis is devastating for an organization.

Playing Games

In troubled entrepreneurial organizations, game playing occurs when employees try to control erratic entrepreneurial behavior. If the organization lacks stability, employees attempt to manipulate the entrepreneur to act or react in certain ways. The entrepreneur, in turn, tries to force employees to follow a particular directive. Both use this gaming technique to achieve their own specific agendas.

Each side usually proffers excuses for indulging in this behavior and claims using such methods is the only way to get the desired results. The use of manipulative methods is proof not only of an organization in trouble due to a lack of trust on both sides but also of a management problem that will grow to unwieldy proportions if left unattended.

Building Trust

Just as trust is the building block of society, the corporate culture constitutes the society in business and must be based on mutual trust and respect. A mistake many parents/entrepreneurs make is to treat their children/organizations as if they were much younger than they actually are.

Parents often demonstrate their misgivings about the capabilities of their children by withholding trust. If parents were to raise their expectations and risk trusting their children, within limits, they would find their children are more apt to behave within acceptable parameters. In the same way, many entrepreneurs tend to regard the companies they have founded as too young and inexperienced to run themselves. They, too, often withhold trust by refusing to delegate or allow others to make decisions.

In one of the developmental phases discussed in this book, the Disassociated Director phase, entrepreneurs often agree to delegate yet keep interfering with decisions they don't participate in making. This represents inconsistent behavior to employees and reaffirms suspicions that the entrepreneur can no longer be trusted. Organizations in this phase of development encounter an impasse. As a result, company growth is stifled or, in some cases, thwarted.

What Does it Take to be Successful?

If most entrepreneurs understood how important it is for everyone to know what is going on, they would most likely take a giant step forward in effectively communicating and overcoming any impasse. If entrepreneurs work with employees, sharing values and creating the vision together, they are able to more readily achieve their corporate mission, or stated goals, and the objectives of the organization.

Additionally, if entrepreneurs recognize their behavior patterns, are alert to the danger signals of "un-CEO-like" behavior, understand how to articulate their vision, embrace core values, and strategically approach decision making and planning, they can develop a leadership style and organizational structure to effectively support themselves, the company and continuous growth.

Entrepreneurial Growth Phases

The four phases of entrepreneurial growth explored in this book and identified for our purposes are:

Phase 1:	*Entrepreneurial Genius*
Phase 2:	*Benevolent Dictator*
Phase 3:	*Disassociated Director*
Phase 4:	*Visionary Leader*

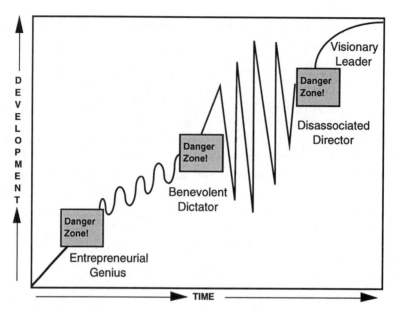

The development of the entrepreneur, and therefore the organization, follows a predictable development pattern. The line illustrates the "stability" or abilities of the entrepreneur in the respective phases.

Most entrepreneurs find themselves locked into the first three phases, often bouncing from one to another as circumstances dictate. Phase 4, Visionary Leader, is where the organization can be effectively led and managed without compromising the entrepreneur's greatest asset—entrepreneurial vision. Research indicates less than 1% of entrepreneurs achieve this final growth phase or are even aware it exists.

What is often missing in the earlier phases—Entrepreneurial Genius, Benevolent Dictator and Disassociated Director—is consistent and systematically planned communication, cooperation and collaboration.

If entrepreneurs acquire professional management skills early enough, via either their own development or that of others, they can bypass much of the pain and frustration of the earlier phases and avoid many of the costly mistakes entrepreneurial ventures often experience. In looking at Abraham Maslow's "Hierarchy of

Needs" paradigm, graduating as quickly as possible to the Visionary Leader phase allows entrepreneurs and organizational members to enjoy higher levels of success and self-actualization.

A Human Growth Analogy

Growth cycles of entrepreneurial organizations are predictable and always intertwined with and dependent on those of the entrepreneur. The initial growth of entrepreneurial organizations is directly proportional to the growth and development of the founding Entrepreneurial Genius. However, the ability to guide a company to higher levels of success is determined by a more sophisticated Visionary Leader's decisions and actions.

To explain this simply, we compare company growth with that of human development as they share common phases and cycles.

Infancy and Entrepreneurial Geniuses

When a company is in its infancy, there is a feeling of family. The entrepreneur, acting as the parent, envisions the newborn company as being the best and the brightest. The entrepreneur feels protective of the organization and its employees; everyone is passionate about the company and wants it to be a winner. The entrepreneur's actions and decisions dictate the infant organization's early growth and development.

As the infant grows and becomes more adept at interpreting feedback from the environment, its capabilities increase. The parent knows the child will walk; it is a natural progression of human development to do so. As the parent anticipates this behavior, the child responds with predictable results. The same occurs in the entrepreneurial organization. The entrepreneur expects great results from the fledgling company and devotes heart and soul to its success. Employees respond by producing excellent results.

But with a fully mobile toddler now actively exploring its environment, the parent is inclined to be more restrictive, believing it is for the child's own good. The parent hovers anxiously saying "don't touch that" and "don't go there" because they feel total responsibility for the child's welfare. They often choose to move objects out of reach or restrain the child rather than educating the child to discern what is safe and what is not.

Childhood and Benevolent Dictators

Unfortunately, if children are completely restricted, they cannot learn and grow. The parent's resistance to allow for that growth eventually creates problems. The propensity to overprotect stifles a child's natural curiosity, so the child quickly learns to compensate by exhibiting uncooperative behaviors.

As leaders/parents, entrepreneurs feel they know best. They tend to become more autocratic—a Benevolent Dictator—telling everyone what to do. They never realize they are inhibiting the organization's progress, just as the parent does who treats the toddler wanting to explore as if everything were hazardous to its health.

Entrepreneurs perceive themselves as caretakers for the company. As the company feels its way through the initial stages of growth, employee needs expand. In response to these increased needs, entrepreneurs often provide what they believe employees should have rather than what they may really need.

Similar to a child who demands independence and balks at discipline, the entrepreneurial organization also desires more freedom. If the limitations are not removed, the organization may begin to challenge the entrepreneur's motives, abilities and authority.

At this point, like any new parent, the entrepreneur becomes confused. Paternalistic behavior that was championed when the company was founded now severely limits organizational growth. The parent hasn't learned to let go and give the child room to grow.

As the child enters puberty and has to cope with the many changes in the world around them, the parent continues to treat the adolescent as a child, not realizing the passage of time means maturity is approaching. In a like manner, the entrepreneur is unprepared to deal with a growing company and anticipate its changing needs.

Adolescence and Disassociated Directors

After a while, the teenager no longer heeds the parent's advice. The parent may try to be rational but eventually ends up being inconsistent, first telling the adolescent to go ahead and drive the family car, then refusing to hand over the keys because they do not trust the teen's judgment. The parent may try to disassociate from all the problems that keep surfacing. Parent and child stop communicating. The young adult is totally without guidance, left to wrestle with their growing pains at a time when direction would be useful but is not available to them.

So, too, there is likely to be disorganization in the adolescent company because the entrepreneur has not established policies, procedures, processes, systems or tasks. Disliking formal structures, most entrepreneurs typically refuse to hold or attend meetings and distance themselves from employees. They take trips and tell the company, "If you're so smart, do it your way." But, true to their entrepreneurial behavior patterns, they come back to the office only to criticize what has been accomplished during their absence.

When company growth outstrips the owner's capacity to manage it, there develops a sense of isolation. The formation of new departments, an increased number of employees and a multitude of new orders adds to the confusion. Because the entrepreneur does not trust employees to run the company and refuses to delegate, the entrepreneur and the organization are probably at the lowest point in their relationship.

Adulthood and the Visionary Leader

Finally, after much soul-searching, the parent may discover that allowing the child some independence, treating them as an adult, and guiding their progress without relinquishing total control, improves the relationship and resolves most of their differences.

Often a parent who wants to earn their child's love and respect will seek counsel from another or identify with a role model. The role model may be someone they consider to be an ideal parent whom they choose to emulate—perhaps a family member, a neighbor, a friend or even a fictional character—and they mimic the successful parenting behavior.

As the role model proves useful, the parent takes the first steps toward nurturing a mutual understanding by communicating with the child. This "talking over our problems" leads to communication on both sides as each develops a greater appreciation for and understanding of the other's position and can, therefore, be more supportive and empathetic.

Had the parent learned this earlier, they could have avoided many unnecessary arguments with the child. By sharing dreams for the future along the way, the two could have enjoyed the exchange and found it much more rewarding and fulfilling.

The parent and child can now work together to resolve their differences without being disagreeable. Trust between the parent and child is restored. The result is a balanced relationship with parent and child collaborating with each other. The parallel in the entrepreneurial organization is that of the entrepreneur who models ideal CEO behavior, acquiring appropriate managers or management skills and learning the techniques needed to carry the company to maturity.

If the entrepreneur and organizational members communicate and trust in each other; if the entrepreneur behaves in a consistent manner and employees know where they fit in; if the needs of employees are met; if everyone cooperates as part of a committed and dedicated team, then the entrepreneur and the organization are more apt to collaborate—the highest level of success—and together create an overall corporate structure that reflects the values of all concerned.

The significant difference between the parent/child and entrepreneur/employee relationship is that employees are adults even when the company is in its infancy. If employees are treated as the adults that they are early in the company's development, preferably from initial start-up, then the organization can grow and reach maturity without experiencing much of the misery that interferes with productivity.

Understanding the Role of Abraham Maslow's Hierarchy of Needs

A crucial skill entrepreneurs can acquire on their way to becoming effective Visionary Leaders is an understanding of human nature and how it affects the development and motivation of their employees. Motivated employees enrich a company; demoralized ones suffocate and destroy it.

What drives employees to be productive and make significant contributions to the organization? Psychologist Abraham Maslow believed human beings are compelled by their very nature to become self-actualized as peak performers. He suggested we all have inner driving forces that compel us to endeavor to reach our full potential.

Human beings share common needs, or fundamental goals, that are achieved through specific motivations and drives. Characteristic of human beings is the desire for something meaningful and challenging in their lives. When one desire is satisfied, another pops up to take its place.

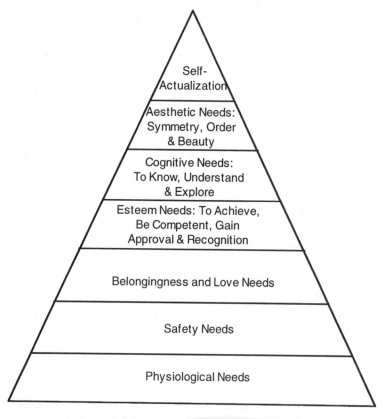

Maslow's Hierarchy of Needs

Physiological needs are at the base of the pyramid. Each successive layer becomes more social in structure and to a greater extent is a learned social need, rather than a need expressing physiological imbalance.

Maslow classified human needs into a hierarchy, or series of steps, expressed visually in the shape of a pyramid and referred to as Maslow's Hierarchy of Needs.

The bottom step encompasses the basic physiological needs necessary to sustain life such as food, water and shelter. If one completed the journey from the bottom to the top, one would finally arrive at self-actualization, or total fulfillment.

As the needs at each level are fulfilled, a person naturally moves up the pyramid to focus on the next step. Upward movement leads to the satisfaction of more intellectual and emotional needs. The higher up one goes, the less they are concerned with basic needs and the more with making a contribution and feeling a sense of purpose.

Entrepreneurs contribute by striving to make the world a better place in which to live. Others may contribute by performing a given task with excellence. In the entrepreneurial organization, all contributions are essential to the success of the enterprise.

Maslow theorized that a person could be truly happy and fulfilled only when they were true to their own nature. When people are forced to work at jobs they loathe, they cannot possibly reach their full potential. Unless they are well suited to what they are doing, they risk feeling restless and dissatisfied.

Some people have a tendency to depend on others to satisfy their needs; others are self-sufficient. Some find satisfaction through external means such as families or employment while others satisfy their own needs internally.

Passionate and independent, most entrepreneurs operate at Maslow's highest level as a natural result of their personality, abilities and talents. They tend to be self-actualized, satisfying their own needs and desires at almost every level, climbing quickly and easily to the pinnacle and bringing into reality their higher selves.

Entrepreneurs have a sense of security and confidence that their new business will flourish which takes care of their safety needs. Their need for belonging and love is satisfied by their position at the helm and their affection for their organizational "family."

Esteem needs are evident in the vision they have of the new product or service. The start-up of the business allows them to challenge, risk, achieve and make a difference while garnering recognition within their industry, business and social environments.

Entrepreneurs satisfy their cognitive needs when they break new ground; find themselves on the forefront of their chosen fields of endeavor; meet challenges head-on; or enjoy the beauty of an idea they have brought to fruition. Some entrepreneurs satisfy these needs by the difference they seek to make in the environment, whether it be in the corporate culture or on a global scale.

The Self-Actualized Entrepreneur

Maslow wrote that average, normal, well-adjusted people are often ignorant of who they are, what they want to become or even how they feel. Those who have reached full potential, on the other hand, have an acute awareness of their own desires, opinions and impulses.

The behavior of self-actualized people is usually consistent, relatively spontaneous, somewhat unconventional, highly ethical and marked by simplicity and naturalness. Self-actualizers are trusting. They dislike artificiality, "playing games," and hypocrisy. Interestingly enough, they are comfortable with their own shortcomings, if not with those of others, because they enjoy incredibly high self-esteem.

Self-actualizers tend to have a mission in life, a vision to fulfill, and a genuine desire to help the human race. Maslow pointed out that these people are self-starters, independent and self-disciplined, working within a framework of values that are broad, not petty.

They make long-term plans and never get so close to a problem they cannot see the "forest for the trees." Self-actualizers gaze at a wider horizon than most and often exhibit a lack of concern over what other people find disturbing, even if those concerns could make life easier not only for the peak performers but for everyone associated with them.

As their basic needs have been met, those at the pinnacle of Maslow's pyramid are motivated to achieve their goals by growth and development whereas non-self-actualizers may be motivated by a sense that they lack something.

Employees strive to have their basic needs gratified; entrepreneurs gratify their own basic needs. As entrepreneurs easily fulfill their own needs, their impulses are directed more toward character expression and growth. In the entrepreneurial organization, this is manifested when the entrepreneur is managing the company professionally and acting as the Visionary Leader.

When entrepreneurs are absorbed in a project or interest, they are inclined to sidestep the rules to which they would otherwise conform. In business, this may be evident when entrepreneur/founders bypass office procedures to achieve their objectives.

Characteristic of entrepreneurs is a penchant for privacy. They find it easy to be aloof and undisturbed by turmoil; most appear to be more objective than other non-actualized people, which helps them to be problem-centered rather than ego-centered. Sometimes entrepreneurs exhibit behavior that is regarded as absent-minded but, in reality, is merely an ability to concentrate to a greater degree than the average person.

This detachment can create problems within an entrepreneurial organization if the behavior is seen as unfriendly or hostile by those who do not comprehend self-actualization. However, if employees understand entrepreneurial behavior patterns, they will likely feel less threatened.

Because self-actualized entrepreneurs are less ego-centered, they are more open to learning, be it from a colleague, a line worker, a professor or even a waiter. Self-confident, they transcend class, race, gender or color and pay less attention to these distinctions than most people do.

As peak performers, self-actualized entrepreneurs are usually great believers in self-autonomy. Within the entrepreneurial organization, this can reveal itself as a belief in self-government, where employees are encouraged to participate in management as a democratic process.

Do these demigods have any defects? Yes, like all human beings, they are not perfect. They can be stubborn, irritating, proud, vain and even ruthless; however, in the business arena, these imperfections may be seen as assets and, in any event, self-actualized entrepreneurs will nevertheless stay within their values whatever their circumstances.

Self-Actualization for the Organization

If entrepreneurs stay within their values, move toward their vision, and understand how every action they take and every word they say affects employees and the ultimate satisfaction of employee needs, the result very well may be excellence in products and services and the best entrepreneurial organization possible.

Early in the development of the company, entrepreneurial commitment, passion and charisma are sufficient to satisfy most employee needs and allow organizational members to reach their full potential. However, as the personality style and nature of the entrepreneur are focused toward self-actualization, they may not realize employees need their support and assistance to move up the pyramid.

Assistance can include benefits such as health insurance, bonus programs or paid personal leave; all of which contribute to the sense of security employees need to work productively. Policies, procedures, processes, systems and tasks are other support measures which permit employees to feel that they are part of the organization and that their personal contribution to the company has value.

All of these factors contribute to employee satisfaction and pride in their work, eventually leading to the development of highly motivated individuals who are capable of producing peak performance. On the other hand, if the entrepreneur neglects to satisfy changing needs, employees are fated to remain at the lower levels.

By focusing on the organization's strengths and delegating to those who can compensate for weaknesses, entrepreneurs can quickly and simply make the transition from Entrepreneurial Genius to Visionary Leader.

Chapter 2

The Phases of Entrepreneurial Growth: From Inspiration through Exasperation

To open a business is very easy;
to keep it open is very difficult.
—Chinese Proverb

The majority of entrepreneurs and entrepreneurial organizations experience a series of easily recognizable developmental phases during their growth that can be aptly characterized as Entrepreneurial Genius, Benevolent Dictator, Disassociated Director and Visionary Leader.

The first three phases are identified by distinct behavioral characteristics and the focus of the organization's energy. The fourth phase is really an ongoing process for managing the entrepreneurial organization to maximize its potential.

As entrepreneurs usually act as the CEOs of their companies, an assumption follows that they possess the inherent skills to run the organization, just as people are assumed to have the intelligence and wisdom to be competent parents.

At certain stages in a company's development, however, it may become evident that management expertise has not kept pace with growth, and entrepreneurs fall behind the maturation of the organization. This phenomenon is referred to as "falling behind the learning curve." In this situation, entrepreneurs can benefit greatly by recognizing and changing ineffective behavioral patterns.

Overview of the Developmental Growth Phases

The Entrepreneurial Genius phase begins with the start-up of the business. During this period, entrepreneurs are very much sales-driven, committed, passionate and charismatic. It is exciting and exhilarating to work for such people.

The general mood in Entrepreneurial Genius organizations is one of hope and optimism. Employees are typically performing at peak levels because their needs are satisfied. They sit at the pinnacle of Maslow's pyramid. Treated as peers by the Entrepreneurial Genius, employees enjoy immense rapport and interaction. There is a feeling of family within the company.

Initially, the euphoria that comes with the introduction of a new product or service prevails. Success happens rapidly, and the company naturally expands. The developing business calls for increased workloads and recruitment of more employees. Soon the sense of being one large family shifts as the needs of the organization change. The fun disappears from the enterprise. Now it is a "real" business, but typically not a very well-managed one.

Entrepreneurs subsequently become obsessed with filling orders and running the growing company, leaving little time to share with employees. Consequently, employees grow disillusioned with this distant leadership style. Although entrepreneurial charisma is still high, it is revealing flaws; charisma can disguise incompetence more effectively than any other character trait or behavior.

Entrepreneurs may now find themselves with a business that is out of control because creativity and passion do not always translate into the appropriate skills needed to make a company function well over time. Entrepreneurs may find that their laser-like attention to gross sales revenues has resulted in a cash-flow crisis. To solve the problem, entrepreneurs turn to the people who know everything there is to know about money: accountants. Unfortunately, this only compounds the problem.

Typically very cautious, accountants may begin by establishing tighter credit policies for customers, subsequently leading to a slowdown in sales. They often restrict expense authorization that, in turn, affects organizational purchasing power.

As accountants are corporate historians, they impose rules and regulations in an effort to track everything. When the organization begins focusing on accommodating the needs of accountants, employees tend to concentrate more on the rules of order than on generating sales and satisfying customer needs.

Eventually this leads to an internal shift in focus. In theory, accountants try to free up more cash to buy more raw materials so the organization can sell more product to produce even more revenue. In an effort to bring order out of the chaos, accountants may exercise too much control, bringing the activities of the organization virtually to a halt.

In an effort to stem the tide of employee discontent aggravated by the restrictive rules and "fix" whatever has gone wrong, entrepreneurs fall into the trap of believing they are the only ones who can solve the problems. After all, "it is their company." Forced into a behavioral change by circumstances, they become paternalistic and domineering, turning into Benevolent Dictators, the second phase.

During this phase of development, the organization will still experience growth if the drive to meet higher needs for achievement and recognition provides enough motivation for everyone to work harder. That motivation must be significant to override the repression and domination of overbearing Benevolent Dictators.

As hard work should equate to appropriate rewards, employees anticipate greater accountability, authority and responsibility. Employees begin to expect and then demand increased input into doing "their" jobs. Entrepreneurs agree with this rationale, but entrepreneurial nature and a recurrent lack of management skills tend to prevent them from letting go. This results in frustrated employees and confused entrepreneurs.

This quandary leads entrepreneurs into the third phase as Disassociated Directors. The passage into this phase is marked by an inability to delegate or trust, along with decreased ego gratification for the founding genius.

Responding to increasing employee demands, entrepreneurs may grudgingly relinquish responsibility without assigning the appropriate accountabilities and authority. Often entrepreneurs have no faith in or understanding of employee capabilities. Even when they do delegate, Disassociated Directors are notorious for continually interfering with decisions others make. Consequently, employees are resentful as well as frustrated.

Predictably unpredictable, the erratic behavior of the entrepreneur compels the company to swing like a pendulum from a sales-driven focus to an operations-driven one and back again. On the plus side of this third phase, these negative entrepreneurial characteristics can produce teamwork and unity among employees as everyone pulls together in an effort to develop more self-reliance. Driving this behavior, of course, is the desire on the part of employees to fulfill their own inner needs on Maslow's pyramid.

Experiencing A Little Discomfort...

The Benevolent Dictator and Disassociated Director phases are often uncomfortable for all concerned. In the second phase, for instance, when entrepreneurs take on the role of Benevolent Dictators, they become unnecessarily autocratic and thwart creativity.

However, these growing pains can engender a desire to seek alternative cures that enrich and reward everyone. Adverse conditions often force people to change, particularly in the case of entrepreneurs who need a significant emotional experience in order to modify behavior. The pain of trying to manage an out-of-control organization usually provides this impetus.

If the foundation of the business is not solid, certain portions of the first three growth phases will be re-enacted over and over again until either a strong foundation develops to support the entire organization or justification for closing the company becomes overwhelmingly evident.

The phases described above represent three of the four phases of entrepreneurial growth. Not every entrepreneur nor entrepreneurial organization is destined to pass through these three phases. However, research indicates aspects of each phase are evident in all entrepreneurial organizations.

If an organization is in the Entrepreneurial Genius phase, an awareness of the subsequent phases can result in the organization taking a short-cut and moving directly to the fourth phase. Others now in the Benevolent Dictator or Dissociated Director phases can identify their status and take steps to remedy the situation and ease the pain, confusion and frustration.

...Then Collecting the Rewards

When an organization has reached managerial maturity, it is in the fourth and most desirable phase of entrepreneurial development—the Visionary Leader phase. In this phase, the organization is purpose-driven with every function directed toward serving clients, customers, vendors and employees.

> *A leader is best*
> *When people barely know he exists,*
> *Not so good when people obey and acclaim him,*
> *Worst when they despise him.*
>
> —Lao-tzu
> *The Way of Life*

The Visionary Leader phase is rewarding because the organization is self-sufficient enough to allow the entrepreneur the freedom to lead without having to assume the demands of day-to-day operational management. In this chapter, we will explore entrepreneurial development and growth through the first three phases. The Visionary Leader phase will be discussed later in Chapter 3.

PHASE 1: ENTREPRENEURIAL GENIUS

Man's mind, stretched to a new idea, never goes back to its original dimensions.

—Oliver Wendell Holmes

Characteristics of this phase include excitement, exhilaration, optimism and hope. The company is new; the entrepreneur is fired up with enthusiasm; products are on-line; and expectations for future success are unbridled.

Entrepreneurial Genius behavior is distinguished by total commitment to the concept of the new business. In this early stage of organizational development, entrepreneurs are like magnets drawing everyone toward the realization of the entrepreneurial dream.

As entrepreneurs establish their business, it is common for them to view the future with a simple, one-dimensional plan—create the commodity and sell it. During this initial phase, entrepreneurs have little patience, time or energy for anything else except the pursuit of more sales.

As they see their dreams become reality and achieve a modicum of success in the marketplace, entrepreneurs generate even more energy, boosting morale throughout the company. With increasingly positive feedback, entrepreneurs move from committed to passionate, attracting even the most cynical to their cause. People are naturally drawn toward these magical people who are destined to change the world.

Easily Satisfying Maslow's Needs

During early stages of the Entrepreneurial Genius phase, employees experience a sense of accomplishment, feel content, and fulfill their highest inner needs. With entrepreneurs treating employees as peers—"We're all in this together! Isn't it great?"—there is an enormous desire to strive for excellence. Negativity and "can't do" attitudes are non-existent; employees receive abundant fulfillment of all their needs.

The majority of entrepreneurs are most comfortable during this phase, when companies are small, values are shared, and everything is positive and upbeat.

As the business usually has only a handful of employees, it is pretty loosely organized. There is little need for rules or structure. With employees assuming responsibility for managing themselves, entrepreneurs can be very tolerant and forgiving of mistakes. A mutual admiration society prevails—entrepreneurs are easy to please and, consequently, extravagant in recognizing employee contributions.

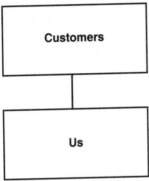

Entrepreneurial Genius Organizational Chart

During the Entrepreneurial Genius Phase, the entrepreneur's focus is on the customer and they view their organization as one entity designed and structured to meet only the needs of their customers.

Confidence in the entrepreneurial dream is profuse. Entrepreneurs engender total trust and treat every staff member as one of an extended family, creating a sense of belonging. Employees feel secure, safe and valued.

An ample supply of approval and recognition are available. If confirmation does not always come readily from entrepreneurs, others outside the organization who wish to associate with such dynamic leadership willingly provide that validation.

With everyone involved in the decision making process, employees' cognitive needs are met as well. This sharing of information about what is going on within the organization permits employees to constantly know and understand how the company is performing.

Consequently, employees are convinced entrepreneurs have Master Plans and that everything will follow accordingly. Their aesthetic needs for order and symmetry are satisfied. At this point, employees are at the highest levels of Maslow's pyramid and perform most effectively.

Focusing on Sales

The start-up phase of a company is often marked by specific factors that eventually affect future growth. For example, entrepreneurs are inclined to focus only on the concept of the product or service and neglect to put in place structure and support systems the organization needs for long-term survival and expansion.

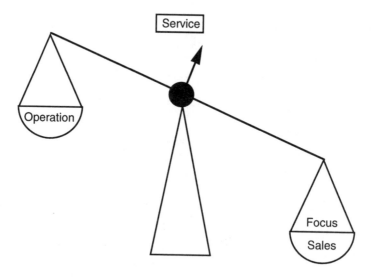

During the Entrepreneurial Genius Phase the entrepreneur and the organization are sales-driven. The entrepreneur over-develops the concept of the product or service and under-develops the structure to support the product or service.

Fledgling companies are usually completely sales-driven with every function geared toward getting the product or service to market. Employees are empowered to make decisions on the spot and take spontaneous action. A "can do" attitude pervades the company. As nothing is considered impossible, everyone becomes resourceful at providing whatever the customer desires.

During the early sales-driven period, most decisions are based on a sales perspective and dictated by the market. The entrepreneur invents, the customer buys. To acquire sales, entrepreneurs willingly do anything including over-promise and under-deliver. Because sales are all-important, this focus brings those in the organization closer together as they scramble to accommodate the wide spectrum of customer requests.

The organization is extremely agile and has tremendous flexibility. Without fixed guidelines, modifications in the product or service correspond with being more responsive to customer needs. Searching for a competitive advantage often results in entrepreneurs granting permission without regard to the feasibility of accomplishing what has been promised.

With expectations high, sales figures remain the overriding concern. Entrepreneurs often see company development and growth simply as an abstract adjunct to all-important sales, forgetting that sales lead company growth. This expansion must be handled as part of organizational development and carries with it a different set of challenges.

The effect is an imbalance; however, at this stage, the imbalance may appear to be only a minor concern. Entrepreneurs continue to over-promise and under-deliver. As the company is new and the entrepreneur so convincing, everyone wants to give the company a fighting chance. Customers don't panic when orders are late; they understand a young business often has growing pains.

Experiencing Growing Pains

As entrepreneurs look for strategies to expand their businesses, they tend to focus too heavily on an increase in revenues as a cure-all for their problems. This over-concentration on one aspect of the business encourages the organization to ignore other equally important functions.

As revenues increase and the company grows, it inevitably leads to a need for more and larger departments. The number and variety of tasks to be handled multiply. Whereas in the start-up stage paperwork was simple to process, now a large order may require completing government forms which further complicates the process. The lack of policies, procedures and systems becomes obvious. This issue will be detailed in later chapters.

At some point, if the entrepreneur stays in this mode, unique hurdles lie ahead. If the business continues to focus on sales without allocating time and resources to product development and research or establishing systems for processing and invoicing orders, the company may find itself short of cash.

If vendors refuse to accept more work without receiving payment on account, entrepreneurs may persuade the vendor that waiting a little longer will be advantageous. Without any conscious level of awareness, entrepreneurs may then promise to compensate this vendor with the same dollars already set aside to pay another — a variation of the old "Robbing Peter to pay Paul" syndrome.

When companies are sales-driven, there are virtually no demands for structure until breakdowns occur. As Entrepreneurial Geniuses encounter problems, they tend to see them as opportunities; and, often the last to seek advice, try to deal with the breakdowns themselves.

Entrepreneurs continue to perpetuate an ineffective process until they feel forced to consult with others. Perhaps for the first time, they may approach accountants to learn what options are available to generate more cash.

Understanding Cash or Credit

The shift in the relationship between accountants and entrepreneurs may begin by simply examining the accumulation of expenses for raw materials due to a massive increase in new sales. Accountants will often suggest establishing credit policies as a means to ensure clients pay in a timely manner, thus creating a way to control and, hopefully, enhance cash flow.

A lack of credit policies can eventually lead to an increase in bad debt or slow payments so accountants are apt to lobby for higher credit standards. Entrepreneurs, by this time, are frustrated with the lack of cash flow and unwittingly agree.

Accountants then institute stricter qualifications for credit and, true to this cautious profession, over-correct the problem, making it extremely difficult for customers to obtain credit and, therefore, buy from the organization. This action directly affects sales, effectively putting accountants in charge of that aspect of the business. In good faith, however, accountants believe they are truly helping the company.

Over-Reacting

Additional problems surface when entrepreneurs delegate credit decisions to accountants who do not have the overall perspective of entrepreneurs, and subsequently implement credit checks that squeeze out existing customers. Entrepreneurs understand the unique needs of their loyal customers enough to go along with those needs; but accountants may not and thus could be responsible for losing valued customers through rigid policies.

Consequently, entrepreneurs may decide to establish structured accounting functions. However, like most entrepreneurs, they continue to over-react. Now the company finds itself engaged in trying to keep up with new systems and procedures while adequately staffing the various divisions needed to operate the business and deliver product.

Employees, instead of pursuing ways of providing better service to customers, find themselves immersed in improving internal systems to ensure the organization is operating properly. The result is a business concentrating on *its* needs rather than on those of the customer.

This change to an internal focus indicates the company and entrepreneur are on the verge of entering the Benevolent Dictator phase of development. An operations-driven company will find itself firmly in the grip of activities focused on how to make the company run efficiently and on doing business for the convenience of the company, not the customer.

For example, a customer may call in and say, "I want to purchase your product." Employees, in a sales-driven organization, would respond quickly by filling the order with a minimum of "formality." However, in the operations-driven organization, the salesperson is apt to respond by telling prospective customers they need to apply for credit, fill out numerous forms and adhere to dozens of policies that technically have value but in reality tend to kill sales.

In many cases, no system has been established for evaluating customer credit requests. The order is further delayed because employees are unsure about payment or terms. However, because sales policies have always been fairly liberal in the past, customers balk. This frustrates both customers and employees. As a result, the sales department is angered and morale sinks to an all-time low.

Often it costs a company more in time and resources to conduct credit checks than the profit they make on the product or service. This over-control is as bad as having no control. A well-thought out policy is needed, not one based upon an emotional response to an immediate problem.

Another pitfall to financial control is the entrepreneurial tendency to believe all revenues are personal property because they "own the company." Good accountants quickly learn to be politically correct, that is, to go along with entrepreneurial demands, often to the detriment of the organization.

It is difficult for any accountant, at this stage, to change an entrepreneur's attitude if they believe gross revenues are bottom line and constitute cash flow. However, accountants do have the entrepreneur's attention and can begin to put in place a series of financial controls to help entrepreneurs better understand where all the money goes.

Shifting to an Operations-Driven Focus

To relieve the cash flow shortage, accountants typically place controls on expenses and purchases. The workings of the organization undergo scrutiny to see where protocols or new controls can be introduced to systematize every function. Entrepreneurs often decide the controls are great, and little by little, are persuaded to establish tighter procedures. With the organization focused on these activities, sales are neglected.

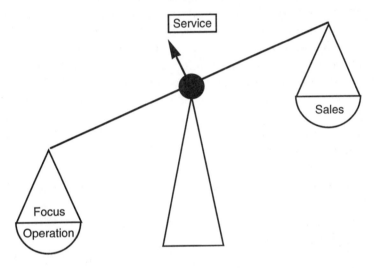

During the Benevolent Dictator phase the focus of the organization becomes inward and towards the operations of the company.

Approaching the Danger Zone

As the organization continues to develop, growing pains may persist. While employees loved the freewheeling Entrepreneurial Genius, they are now faced with a leader who insists on controlling every detail. Employees look to entrepreneurs to move the company out into the future, not to manage the minute daily tasks. This behavior belittles entrepreneurs in the eyes of their employees and can cause confusion.

Even when entrepreneurs possess the skills to manage effectively, employees expect them to act like leaders, not line workers. Yet, entrepreneurs sincerely believe they are responding to employee demands for management in this way.

In reality, the work force needs self-management and not that imposed by the company founder. Employees want their own authority, accountabilities and responsibilities. Entrepreneurs often respond to such requests by informing employees that they—entrepreneurs—will handle everything so that they—employees—do not have to worry about anything.

At this stage, both entrepreneurs and organizational members have undergone an unwelcome transition. Dissension becomes widespread. The "happy-go-lucky" attitude that pervaded the organization during the start-up phase is no longer apparent.

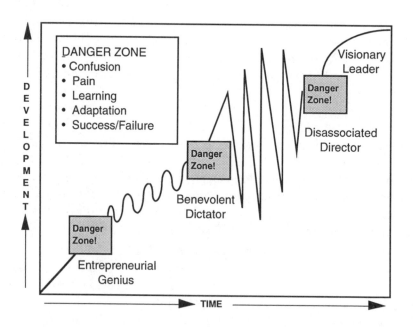

As entrepreneurs move from phase to phase they enter a "danger zone." Each danger zone changes the focus of the entrepreneur, and the organization.

It is evident entrepreneurs and organizational members have reached the "danger zone." Employees feel their needs have not been met and ask the founder/parent figure to remedy the situation. This signals entrepreneurs are entering the second phase of organizational development and becoming full-fledged Benevolent Dictators.

PHASE 2: BENEVOLENT DICTATORS

If you want a thing done well, do it yourself.

—Napoleon Bonaparte

The behavioral switch to Benevolent Dictator is an identifiable progression following the Entrepreneurial Genius stage with entrepreneurs becoming more like parents telling their children what to do, when and how, and dictating the criteria. Characteristic of this phase is a suffocating domination on the part of entrepreneurs.

Entrepreneurs control every function in the company, make every decision and are convinced this style of management is for everyone's own good. Both sides engage in strategies to satisfy their own needs and agendas.

As Benevolent Dictators use more force to bring everyone into conformity, employees often rebel. The ensuing struggle can wreak havoc and inhibits the development of the organization and the entrepreneur.

Drawing by Ross © 1981. The New Yorker Magazine, Inc.

*"It's the multitude, and they're <u>not</u> singing
'For He's a Jolly Good Fellow.'"*

Identifying Parents and Children

Whereas initially entrepreneurs shared thoughts and ideas liberally with their employee "family," now they keep their own counsel, which, in their opinion, is legitimate behavior.

As the business grows, employee demands increase. Entrepreneurs, sensitive to employee needs, respond as parents would to their children—assuring them they will be taken care of. This response is not what employees are seeking. They want independence, even autonomy, but entrepreneurs won't listen or refuse to understand.

Benevolent Dictators believe completely in themselves, feeling an obligation to care for and take action that is in the best interests of employees. This mentality indicates entrepreneurs take for granted the child (the young company) is still in the playpen and not ready to have any unsupervised mobility.

Not so long ago, employees blindly followed the Pied Piper entrepreneur and trusted in where the organization was headed.

But success creates a different game, and no one has taken the time to explain the new rules. One of the biggest mistakes entrepreneurs make is continuing to run a burgeoning business as if it were still a small enterprise.

Similar to the development of children whose parents are reluctant to release them from their apron strings as they grow older, entrepreneurs often refuse to acknowledge that the small company is now a large operation in need of both management and leadership.

In essence, Benevolent Dictators manage companies for what they were, not for what they will be. They are mired in the past, trying to resolve new problems with old solutions like parents attempting to apply an obsolete curfew to teenagers. Entrepreneurs have not kept pace with the growth of their offspring.

To their credit, entrepreneurs are usually consciously aware when things are not right within the organization; but, often lacking management skills, they have little knowledge of how to correct or even identify the problems. So entrepreneurs do what they do best—they try to take care of everything themselves. They usually treat symptoms rather than looking for the real causes.

Designating the "Identified Patient"

The "identified patient" syndrome is familiar in young companies. This syndrome occurs when entrepreneurs or employees point fingers for faltering sales and disorganization in the company on individuals or on a deficiency such as, "If we only had a decent telephone system, all our problems would disappear" or "If we only had four-color sales brochures, we'd stand out more from our competition."

Everyone is looking for a "patient" on whom to place the blame for current difficulties. Such comments are symptoms, not cures. It is probable there are several reasons for a decrease in sales, but identifying one particular person or thing as the "patient" shows a lack of perspective.

An element of panic is usually present at this time because entrepreneurs are afraid control of the organization is slipping away from them. The enterprise has become unmanageable. The protective parent is confronted by a rebellious young adult. Another sign the Entrepreneurial Genius has transitioned to a Benevolent Dictator is an inclination to over-manage and under-lead, becoming "Vice President of Everything."

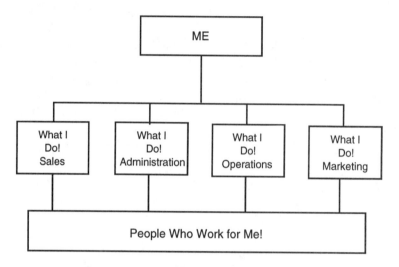

Benevolent Dictator Organization Chart

This organizational chart clearly shows the entrepreneur as "in charge" of everything, and signifies that the entrepreneur and the organization are internally focused.

Living in the Past

With continued growth and expansion, entrepreneurs become more removed from the day-to-day operations of the company. Disenchanted, entrepreneurs desire to return to the "good old days" of the Entrepreneurial Genius phase when they were considered great by just about everyone's standards.

Entrepreneurs and their organizations grow farther and farther apart. No longer receiving the positive feedback that ignited their passion, entrepreneurial egos suffer. The new demands of management are definitely not fun, so entrepreneurs attempt to take the company back to its former glory. Retreating to an earlier phase is perilous to the organization and can cripple the company. It is like asking a teenager to revert to infancy—both have passed the point of no return.

Some entrepreneurs try to go back anyway. Unfortunately, this significant but natural shift in behavior results in turning them into full-fledged Benevolent Dictators rather than in reviving their Entrepreneurial Genius.

If entrepreneurs take the organization back to a former level of comfort and competence, the organization will never develop the skills it will need to successfully meet the demands of the future. By reverting to past behaviors, entrepreneurs can inadvertently create dysfunctional organizations just as easily as parents can create dysfunctional families.

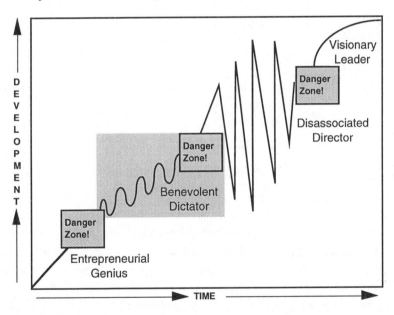

Entrepreneurial organizations in this phase can function indefinitely but only to the level of "incompetence" of the founder.

Turning Defeat into Victory

The primary reason for the wish to recapture the Entrepreneurial Genius ego-gratification days is a growing sense of mistrust and apathy within the organization. Employee attitudes have changed; everything is different. Although this situation may cause entrepreneurs to become defensive and even belligerent, this shift in employee attitude can be leveraged into an advantage.

As the organization grows, employee expectations evolve from those of family members into those of a community. In the Entrepreneurial Genius phase, employee needs are fulfilled. They are peak performers. In the Benevolent Dictator phase, employees have no way to fulfill these inner needs because entrepreneurs no longer give them recognition via promotions and raises nor delegate accountabilities, authority or responsibilities.

A case in point is a five-year old company with six levels of management whose entrepreneur/owner still insists on personally making decisions as to whether any employee is entitled to take a day off. This Benevolent Dictator's paternalistic behavior precludes employees from making decisions and participating in company business. Thus employee self-esteem drops. They no longer feel part of the organization. Employees find themselves consumed in a search to satisfy their basic needs.

Locating Blue Skies on the Horizon

In some organizations, employees are able to check entrepreneurial behavior and manage the business themselves because they are so fiercely motivated to meet their own individual needs. If entrepreneurs are wise enough or fortunate enough to hire competent people, those people can be strong and learn the necessary skills to help the company. Yet, without entrepreneurial leadership, employees may find it difficult to develop the company to its full potential.

In fact, the uncooperative atmosphere should put entrepreneurs on notice that changes are unavoidable. Entrepreneurs can seize the opportunity of employee unrest to introduce appropriate organizational structures and create better management supports.

Descending the Pyramid

Whereas in the Entrepreneurial Genius stage employees' needs were met at the highest level of Maslow's pyramid of self-actualization, an over-controlled company is no longer a safe haven, and causes employees who were exceptional workers to become uncertain and afraid.

With the influx of a larger work force, the feeling of belonging may be lost. Esteem needs are often ignored, and cognitive needs also suffer during the Benevolent Dictator stage because there is little communication, due to entrepreneurial preoccupation with tasks.

Employees find themselves at ground zero, where they must begin the painful climb back up. Company growth, almost without doubt, is the culprit. While increased sales typically lead to expansion and employees are asked to assume more duties, organizations experience turmoil or discontent because entrepreneurs have not paid attention to the crucial component of organizational structure.

Most entrepreneurs are wary of anything resembling bureaucracy, a word that has a negative connotation for them. They are reluctant to create a plan, even though their growing business is becoming chaotic without one. In fact, a great number of people in the company may not even be aware of what the organization is striving to achieve.

Just as children continually challenge their parents' skills, employees may begin to test entrepreneurial management abilities. Because entrepreneurs tend to make "off-the-cuff" decisions, they often neglect to consult with senior executives and fail to establish policies and procedures, undermining the very essence of what made the company successful initially.

Expansion means many decisions must be made on a strategic, long-term basis. However, it is difficult for entrepreneurs to handle this type of decision making. They are more accustomed to making emotional, spontaneous decisions in response to immediate needs in the company or the marketplace. Although they are futurists, entrepreneurs are inclined to look at short-term solutions in their zeal for instantaneous results, and often lose their focus on the future as they become preoccupied with day-to-day operations.

As the organization seems to be in chaos, aesthetic needs demand attention. Disorder adversely affects our need for symmetry. Esteem needs drive employees to demand approval. They count on having opportunities to gain recognition to satisfy their cognitive needs. With little delineation of duties, however, and no departmental structures, there is no vehicle to allow for that acknowledgment.

Additionally, some workers may expect financial rewards for handling increased workloads; others may believe they should receive promotions or become managers. Soon employees begin to credit the growth and success of the company to their own individual diligence and hard work.

This situation does offer an opportunity for the organization to "cut the cord" from Benevolent Dictator domination. With capable senior management, employees can form teams and work as cohesive units, thus gaining some semblance of independence. While this system is only a stop-gap remedy, it can at least provide employees with a temporary means to satisfy their needs and ensure they can adequately defend their position on Maslow's pyramid.

Assuming Financial Experts Will Fix Everything

When the organization demands a flood of responses from the founder/parent figure, entrepreneurs may endeavor to manage the growing business more effectively. Eventually, entrepreneurs seek the counsel of financial experts to sort out the money matters, which seem to be of the highest priority and the source of the most pain.

Financial experts are usually very proficient in handling money issues. Consequently, entrepreneurs often assume anything these people touch will improve. Because these external experts may be effective at solving the fiscal crisis, entrepreneurs may perceive them as having the capacity to handle everything else that is wrong with the company.

As a result, entrepreneurs turn to the financial experts for advice and are counseled on how to "take control." This decision is often a mistake because financial experts—accountants—are paid to be historians; they deal with what has happened, not with what should happen. They look at revenues and how they were disbursed—functions that took place in the past.

They operate under traditional guidelines of economic scarcity and limitation. Entrepreneurs, on the other hand, are visionaries that need to operate in the future. Thus entrepreneurs and financial wizards work from significantly different perspectives—one forward, one back—and their partnership creates further confusion for entrepreneurs.

A signal entrepreneurs need to examine their attitude toward financial affairs is an overriding interest in the gross income rather than the bottom line—the net income. Entrepreneurs derive a false sense of security from the larger figure only to be given a reality check when they learn cash flow has dried up.

Often, that's when entrepreneurs hand over control to accountants, whose single, narrow focus and risk-averse mentality can prove ruinous. Accountants are usually inclined to discourage any moves that could be a risk to the organization. They are naturally and understandably over-cautious, tending to institute fiscal policies that are far too restrictive.

Running a Risky Business

Entrepreneurs, on the other hand, are natural risk-takers, having unrivaled self-confidence. The willingness to risk is what allowed entrepreneurs to lead their companies to this point. But, as they attempt to control the next phases of development and eliminate risk, they sign a death warrant for the organization.

As entrepreneurial organizations grow, their ability to deal with adversity should increase accordingly. Many entrepreneurs try to shield their companies from problems and absorb the "pain" themselves. This strategy of "saving the company" is, in reality, destructive as entrepreneurs are inclined to make hasty, uninformed decisions to relieve their discomfort quickly.

Entrepreneurs may believe the pain can be alleviated by taking it on—by making all the decisions—but this is only a short-term solution to a long-term problem and typically results in a number of "it seemed like a good idea at the time" decisions.

Entrepreneurial security springs from a belief in their own abilities; they only understand that particular perspective. Employee security is derived from position and a belief in and dependence on the organizational structure. If employees didn't have this need, they would more than likely be entrepreneurs themselves.

During the Entrepreneurial Genius phase, employees were encouraged to take risks. The ability to create risk-prone environments allowed entrepreneurs to grow the organization. Yet, as the organization develops and entrepreneurs become Benevolent Dictators and then Disassociated Directors, these environments cease to exist. This shift, in turn, affects all the other needs. Attempting to control the expanding company and eliminate all risk jeopardizes the very safety it is meant to secure.

Employees are unwilling during the Benevolent Dictator phase to stick their necks out because the reward for doing so is no longer present. On the other hand, entrepreneurs are frustrated with employees because of their seeming unwillingness to take any action on their own initiative.

Entrepreneurial organizations can function *ad infinitum* in the Benevolent Dictator phase. However, if this is the case, growth will always be limited and rewards non-existent for both entrepreneurs and the organization.

PHASE 3: DISASSOCIATED DIRECTORS

*A boss's mere expression of an opinion can be interpreted as a
decision—even a direct order—by a staff caught in the clutches
of risk avoidance.*

—R. Alec Mackenzie

The Disassociated Director phase is truly confusing and
frustrating for all concerned. Characteristics of this phase include
distrust, inconsistencies, erratic mood swings, and an inability to
delegate or let go.

When employees finally rebel during the Benevolent Dictator
phase, entrepreneurs quickly learn the organization is not, cannot,
and does not want to be dependent on them for every decision. As
a result, their egos can no longer be gratified through association
with the company.

Most entrepreneurs do not know what to do with the
alienation they feel. Many attempt to default to what they have
always done before; however, by this time, many employees have
begun to essentially ignore entrepreneurs, further adding to their
pain and confusion.

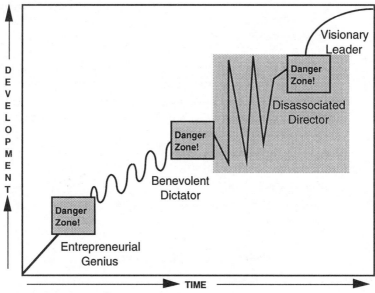

*Entrepreneurs in this phase are erratic and inconsistent and feel isolated from
their own organizations.*

Disassociated Directors often claim they will remove themselves from the day-to-day running of the organization and hand over the reins to professional managers. Unfortunately, they can't resist meddling, and in a short period of time, are back running the company "their" way.

Occasionally, employees respond by developing systems that circumvent Disassociated Director behavior. If employees are committed, they develop a sense of self and can become peak performers. In spite of problems, the company may still be experiencing success. However, continued organizational growth forces a change in employee needs once again.

By permission of Johnny Hart and Creators Syndicate, Inc.

At the initial stages of this phase, most entrepreneurs, realizing there must be a shift, vacillate between Benevolent Dictator and Dissociated Director behaviors. They are consistently inconsistent—issuing directives, only to rescind them in the next breath.

Employees begin to wonder whether the entrepreneur's new plans are "discussions for possibility," "discussions for direction," "discussions for decisions," or literally "marching orders." Needless to say, the organization is no longer sales- or operations-driven—it is absolutely confusion-driven.

Desiring Independence

Successfully meeting adversity in any form increases employee competence and confidence. Just as children progress from crawling to walking through a series of trial-and-error experiences, so employees feel a need to move ahead in their development.

Children achieve new mobility and freedom when they learn to ride a bike. That same mobility presents problems for parents who have neither foreseen nor planned for this new set of circumstances and are ill-equipped to handle the child's increased independence or its variables.

When employees are forced to take action on their own and make decisions in spite of rather than because of entrepreneurs, they naturally yearn for greater independence. They may feel hesitant about striking out on their own; but after having experienced the rush of adrenaline, they want more.

Unfortunately, those closest to the entrepreneur are usually reluctant at this stage to offer advice or a broader perspective because the sense of family has disappeared. They no longer feel close and hesitate to express their opinions, mimicking a childish reluctance to confide in or reveal any secrets. Additionally, the sense of trust is deteriorating.

Usually at some point in every child's development, they begin to trust their peers more than they trust their parents. By the same token, employees now begin to trust each other more than they trust the entrepreneur, and the two have practically become "enemies."

This shift in trust is regarded as a cautionary signal flag in the developmental process. Employees are now busy building their own little empires within the organization so they can regain the safety, security, and sense of belonging they enjoyed during the Entrepreneurial Genius stage.

Return Me to Where I Was!

Employees convince one another they can do the job "better than the boss;" and, in many instances, they can. Esteem needs drive employee motivation, and organizational members begin to discuss what they would do and how they would do it if it were their company. They fulfill their cognitive needs as they build order, symmetry and structure into their work lives.

Unfortunately, every decision they make is reversed by ineffective entrepreneurs, causing employees to become frustrated. Moreover, customers and vendors see chinks appearing in the organizational armor and prepare their own game plan accordingly.

Feeling Confusion-Driven

Entrepreneurial behavior at this point continues to be confusing to the organization. Consequently, entrepreneurs may encounter management theories like "Management by Objectives" and attempt to institute some new policies. Yet, in essence, entrepreneurs haven't fully developed the skills to manage by anything.

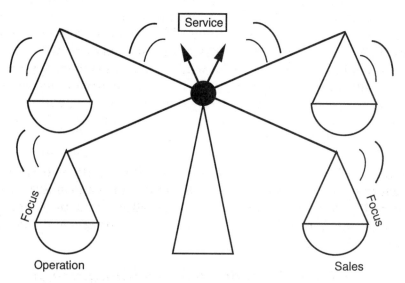

The entrepreneur and the organization are swinging wildly from operations to sales driven, becoming confusion driven.

Employees are uncomfortable with the Disassociated Director phase and its accompanying artificial management style. They dig in their heels, refusing to comply with even the simplest requests.

The infant is learning to walk but the parent won't let go of its hand—so it sits on the floor and howls.

As working conditions deteriorate, employees agitate to be promoted to positions of responsibility, but Disassociated Directors stubbornly refuse to relinquish control of the company. Entrepreneurs are still motivated individuals but the expectations of new recruits, the resentment of veteran employees, and internal changes affecting external factors, such as customers, sufficiently drain their energy.

Realizing the pendulum has swung too far in one direction, entrepreneurs now seek to restore the balance by swinging the pendulum back too far in the opposite direction. Midway in the pendulum swing the organization may establish some policies and procedures, but these often get out of hand and become overly restrictive. The natural tendency, then, is to go back to being sales-driven, with the result that the pendulum continues to swing back and forth recklessly between the two extremes.

A common situation, these wild pendulum swings appear to be a natural part of growth in any entrepreneurial enterprise— with entrepreneurs first being obsessive about selling the product or service, then compensating to correct that attitude by becoming compulsive about operations.

This devastating pattern, which seems to be inevitable, can be avoided if entrepreneurs make a significant shift in behavior. Instead of reacting emotionally to the many turns a business takes, swinging abruptly from sales to operations and back again, entrepreneurs can pick a leverage point to create some balance between the two.

Assigning Authority, Accountability, and Responsibility

Some entrepreneurs may now have abdicated all their work responsibilities to others. However, since neither the accountability nor authority was assigned at the same time, those to whom entrepreneurs have delegated the responsibility are blocked. Entrepreneurs direct employees to go ahead and do what they think best, then withhold the authority organizational members need to actually accomplish the tasks.

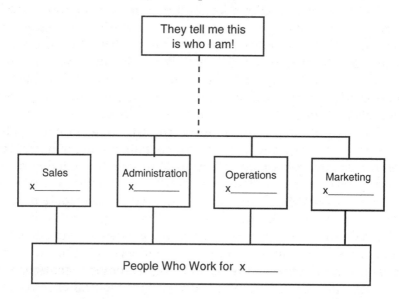

Dissassociated Director Organization Chart

Clearly shows the entrepreneur feeling isolated and others taking "some" functional responsibility.

When entrepreneurs return from "business trips" and conclude the company is not being run to their liking, they often become critical of what has been happening and say, "Well, I would have done this differently ..." and contest every decision made in their absence.

Identifying the False-Start Syndrome

One sure indication entrepreneurs are in the Disassociated Director phase is the appearance of the "false-start" syndrome. In this instance, entrepreneurs will make a decision, contradict themselves, then, in their confusion, replace the first decision with a completely different one. As their behavior appears totally inconsistent, no one depends on anything they say or do.

As Wilson L. Harrell discussed in a *Success Magazine* article, this situation can be likened to primitive cultures where barbarians led the charge into battle—burning and pillaging as they went. After the land had been conquered, farmers moved in to cultivate the land and plant seed. But as soon as the land flourished again, the barbarians returned to burn and pillage once more, offsetting the farmers' endeavors in a never-ending cycle.

So, too, entrepreneurs tend to return after they have supposedly let go and interfere with management, destroying morale and even creating crises so they can feel needed as the glorious conqueror and included again. Entrepreneurs may be well-qualified to lead the charge, but they need to appreciate when to step back and permit others to show the way.

Joseph Francis, entrepreneur and chairman of The Barbers, a publicly-held franchise company, went through this transition several times. Francis decided to bring in senior executives who worked very hard at creating a corporation that far exceeded his expectations. He even hired a president to run his organization in spite of the fact that Francis himself was very successful and had been responsible for the company grossing revenues of more than $6 million.

Although the president he hired increased the company revenues to $17 million, Francis differed with the president in management philosophies. They didn't share the same values; and frankly, Francis wasn't ready to let go. Repeatedly, they battled over policies and strategies. Francis exhibited Disassociated Director behavior by bringing in a president to run the show and then second-guessing this professional manager, continually countermanding his decisions.

Francis finally decided to fire his president and take the job back himself. The franchisees, however, held an emergency meeting and reached consensus. They told Joseph Francis, "If you come back in and run the organization, we will fight you all the way. We do not believe you possess the skills to be our company president."

The Board of Directors then forced Francis to hire another individual as president—someone with whom Francis shared similar values and who was strong enough in their own right to prevent Francis from demonstrating Disassociated Director behavior.

The company is now far more successful because Francis was given the mandate to do what he does best—create new and diverse businesses. The efforts and focus of Francis' true talents are evidenced by The Barbers recent opening of offices in the former USSR.

Very few entrepreneurs can "unplug" and give up control. If qualified senior managers have not been recruited and day-to-day control turned over in the Benevolent Dictator phase, it will be even more difficult for entrepreneurs to do so during the Disassociated Director phase.

Developing a Foxhole Mentality

Entrepreneurs are loathe to let go which is the biggest obstacle to their personal growth and a major developmental hurdle. Entrepreneurs like to have the last word on every decision and action. They don't realize the inability to step back limits the growth of the very enterprise they wish to have succeed. They tend to perpetuate this self-defeating behavior by their stubborn unwillingness to delegate to others.

Various reasons surface for the inability to delegate— entrepreneurs contend, "It's not the right time," or "The manager lacks experience to handle the project," or "No one understands the client like I do." Each reason exposes entrepreneurial fears and limitations projected into the future. When people have responsibility without the accompanying accountability or authority, they develop a foxhole mentality and practice the art of avoidance—staying out of trouble at all costs.

Deciding to Freeze, Flee, or Fight

Any time an organization finds itself in the Disassociated Director phase, employees will do only the bare minimum to get by because everyone is unsure about what to do or where to go next. Thus, the organization reaches a "fear plateau" with three options:

- *Freeze*
- *Flee*
- *Fight*

If employees choose to freeze in place, fearful of making any moves, nothing gets done. Paralysis within the organization becomes rampant.

If employees choose to flee, they often end up leaving the company. Workers become so frustrated with the inconsistent behavior of the entrepreneur, lack of opportunity for promotion or absence of recognition, they bail out in expectation of the ship eventually sinking. Replacing organizational members can be extremely expensive and time-consuming, delaying progress and growth, and even resulting in the acquisition of a "revolving door" reputation.

Fight—the last option—to keep the company afloat, is obviously preferable to the other two. Unfortunately, the fight tends to be internal with entrepreneurs and employees battling each other rather than external, aimed at competitors.

If an organization has limited resources—time, energy and money—and if 80% of its energy is wasted on internal problems, then only 20% is left to deal with the real issues such as:

- *How do we work together to provide what is in the best interest of our customers?*
- *Where is our market niche?*
- *How can we improve our products and provide superior service?*
- *How do we contend with new competitors?*

Suffering from the Airplane Syndrome

As Disassociated Directors, entrepreneurs are particularly susceptible to two phenomena. The first is called the "Airplane

Syndrome." In this instance, entrepreneurs confide their business problems to fellow airline passengers and accept whatever advice they receive as gospel rather than seeking the counsel of company managers and personnel who have a vested interest in the success of the organization.

Attending the "Band-Aid" Seminar

A second phenomenon that usually bodes ill for the organization is the "Management Seminar Syndrome." As Disassociated Directors, entrepreneurs are under-utilized and often find they have time on their hands so they attend management seminars to develop the skills they need to become more effective managers.

Nothing is more dangerous in an organization than a person who has just returned from a one-day management seminar, especially if that person has decision making powers and the authority to implement those decisions.

Even though entrepreneurs are likely to try out the new ideas from the seminar, the concepts may be fragmented in several different directions. Unfortunately, most of the changes don't make any sense or endure for any length of time. Typically, the staff reports back, "We tried your methods; they don't work for us." In reality, entrepreneurs probably only focus on a specific piece of the subject matter presented and therefore fail to communicate and implement all of the necessary components.

Some entrepreneurs think, "I can do this better than the experts." They dabble in a little of this and some of that—a piece of *One-Minute Manager*, a dollop of *Leadership Management*, and a slice of *Management by Objectives*. Finally the organization is sufficiently bewildered and employees respond with, "See, we told you, you are irrational."

Learning is a process not an event—implementation of new ideas can only occur when everyone understands the "process".

—Roy F. Cammarano

Doubting Thomases

In the Entrepreneurial Genius phase, entrepreneurs look for what is right with the company; in the Disassociated Director phase, they look for what is wrong. This attitude stifles creativity within the entrepreneurial enterprise and consequently hampers growth. As Disassociated Directors, entrepreneurs become skeptical and test resolve saying, "Prove it to me!" challenging managers to justify their every action and idea.

By this time, organizational members are not inclined to try and prove anything. Their reluctance to play the game furthers the entrepreneurial "I am right" attitude. Employees desperately feel a need to take pride in their accomplishments in order to satisfy their higher needs; however, few entrepreneurs in this phase can give positive feedback and, unless trained, tend to hog all the credit themselves for any corporate achievements.

During this stagnant stage, the following frustrating scenario typically unfolds:

"We ought to do it this way but they won't let us, we have to do it their way," employees complain.

"No, you don't" entrepreneurs fire back. "I don't care which way you handle it as long as we get results."

But entrepreneurial behavior belies the words. How entrepreneurs communicate is a truer indicator of their disposition than what they say. Employees learn quickly that when they make a decision or initiate a plan during the Disassociated Director phase, entrepreneurs can't and won't resist second-guessing them.

As employees gain self-esteem and become better performers, entrepreneurs naturally expect exceptional behavior from them. However, if entrepreneurial behavior is inconsistent, employee self-esteem is endangered and, consequently, they do not perform to expectations.

Dissension between entrepreneurs and employees creates another hazard. Entrepreneurs begin to doubt themselves and wonder if they can ever master the skills needed to become successful leaders of their businesses. They may even decide they don't enjoy management and look for someone they trust to manage on their behalf.

If entrepreneurs fail to delegate to competent managers or acquire those skills themselves, they will be compelled to take charge yet again. This may reassert their leadership position but inevitably they will slip back to the Entrepreneurial Genius or Benevolent Dictator phases. It is easy to track this backward slide from Disassociated Director to Benevolent Dictator by monitoring the amount of disturbance entrepreneurs are creating for the organization.

Reversing Roles

During either the Benevolent Dictator or Disassociated Director phase of organizational growth, entrepreneurs must be forced into making a paradigm shift that allows the organization to establish its own identity. Organizational members must, in effect, reverse roles and act as parents while entrepreneurs learn this new part in the script.

The staff will have to deal with entrepreneurial impatience, but this stage can be brief. Entrepreneur and employees should realize that initially there will be subtle changes rather than dramatic shifts and that the slow process should not only be tolerated, it must be embraced.

Taking Time to Consider Other Perspectives

Early in their businesses, entrepreneurs will benefit if they take time to consider the company's growth from a variety of perspectives, many of which may be quite diverse from their own. While entrepreneurs look at exceeding sales projections, employees are concerned with job security and competency.

If no strategic plan for development exists, employees may sense growth doesn't necessarily equal promotions or increased responsibilities, and therefore some of their higher needs will not be satisfied.

Customers and vendors have yet another perspective of the company's growth. If an organization is too busy to handle timely invoicing because few or no systems and procedures have been established, it is destined to lose business. Expansion and success may be viewed with alarm as people find it increasingly difficult to place orders or receive payment on accounts.

Companies tend to duplicate mistakes rather than learn from them, expecting a variety of outcomes from the same situation. This process wastes time and energy. As author Rita Mae Brown suggests:

Insanity is doing the same thing over and over again expecting different results.

Similarly, many entrepreneurs find themselves trapped in the first three phases destined to repeat them over and over again. However, managing the organization as a Visionary Leader, the fourth phase, ensures that both the entrepreneur and the organization grow and prosper together.

Chapter 3

Visionary Leadership:
Communication, Cooperation and Collaboration

A leader is best when people barely know he exists . . . when his work is done, his aim fulfilled, they will say we did it ourselves.

—Lao-tzu

Characterized by communication, cooperation and collaboration, the Visionary Leader phase can fulfill the entrepreneurial dream of creating and leading a dynamic company that operates smoothly and successfully.

The Visionary Leader phase exposes entrepreneurs to a powerful leadership and management process that installs and maintains a purpose-driven organization. This phase establishes a new corporate environment and provides entrepreneurs with a more effective way to run their companies.

The first chapters of this book described the entrepreneurial development process and behavior patterns during Entrepreneurial Genius, Benevolent Dictator and Disassociated Director phases of company growth. A significant portion of the two previous chapters also focused on the importance of Maslow's Hierarchy of Needs—how people are compelled to satisfy their inner drives and how needs satisfaction affects employee and organizational performance.

This chapter outlines the components of the Visionary Leader phase and illustrates how entrepreneurial behavior can be used to realize "the dream" of a well-run, prosperous organization. It also focuses on why it is crucial for entrepreneurs to recognize and modify their own ineffective behaviors in order to accelerate the developmental process.

This chapter also explains the interconnectedness of all of the book's concepts and how those concepts relate to each other, especially the "Three Cs" of entrepreneurial transformation—communication, cooperation and collaboration.

"But I Was More Comfortable in the Earlier Phases"

Time after time, entrepreneurs find themselves repeating the Entrepreneurial Genius, Benevolent Dictator and Disassociated Director phases of entrepreneurial growth unable to surmount problems and frustrations once and for all.

While the vision still burns brightly, passion runs high, and commitment remains firm, many entrepreneurs don't understand nor do they appreciate where they lack appropriate behaviors, skills and/or leadership to create the organization of their dreams.

Thus, entrepreneurs find themselves reiterating the same mistakes until:

- *they fail and the business dies*
- *they sell the company and pursue other interests*
- *they recognize ineffective behaviors*
- *the "pain" of running a dysfunctional organization motivates them to make needed changes*
- *they determine they are committed to producing different results*
- *they seek out and hire competent professional managers with objective perspectives.*

Many entrepreneurs indulge in repetitive behavior because it is familiar territory for them. They justify their actions because the company has accomplished a great deal in spite of their often erratic and inconsistent behaviors. They see no reason to change if they "got this far being who they are." What's worse is that this perception has been continually reinforced during the earlier stages of development.

Unfortunately, when organizations grow without parallel development on the part of entrepreneurs or appropriate professional management, an ineffective organization results. However, entrepreneurs rarely recognize that the fault lies within themselves.

When entrepreneurs realize the organization is really just matching and mirroring their behaviors, they can better understand their role in creating the culture and setting the pace. When entrepreneurs are able to correlate problems directly to their own behaviors, they will be much more open to making the modifications necessary to move the enterprise forward.

However, most entrepreneurs find it is easier to return to the mode of behavior they are most comfortable with rather than trying something new or different that is threatening or intimidating. Thus entrepreneurs are apt to revert back to an Entrepreneurial Genius, where they were inspired and admired, even though the company has progressed well past the initial growth stage and little possibility exists for the entrepreneur to recreate this perceived Garden of Eden.

Entrepreneurial Geniuses give birth to companies that are sales-driven. Benevolent Dictators attempt to manage companies that are operations-driven. While companies of Disassociated Directors are absolutely confusion-driven, Visionary Leaders guide companies that are service- or purpose-driven. Regrettably, only a small percentage of organizations have entrepreneurs at the helm who have attained competency as Visionary Leaders.

Entrepreneurs need not remain trapped in the first three phases where organizations are destined to fall short of their full potential. It is possible for entrepreneurs to switch to the fourth phase with an understanding and the implementation of technologies and tools provided in later chapters.

The Vital Equation:
Desire + Determination = Capability

Most entrepreneurs have the capacity to become effective Visionary Leaders provided they possess the desire and determination to develop their own skills or the willingness to allow others who exhibit those qualities to manage in their stead. Most entrepreneurs are motivated to use their capabilities if they can internalize and understand how the concepts discussed in this book apply to them specifically.

Too often, however, the motivation to change comes from the avoidance of pain. Entrepreneurs may try something they don't understand completely in order to alleviate the pain quickly. This "band-aid approach" rarely works but entrepreneurs will attribute the fault to the approach rather than recognizing the implementation of it was the culprit.

Under stress, people retreat to familiar behavior patterns or "comfort zones." Here, they can depend on predictable outcomes resulting from specific actions. Therefore, they feel safe in spite of the fact that, time after time, those behaviors and choices fail to elicit the desired results.

Entrepreneurs shifting to Visionary Leaders are often surprised at how relatively painless the transition really is. The passage into this phase allows them to eliminate the problems and frustrations of the first three and lead a company better qualified to meet the challenges of the future and positioned to achieve success beyond their expectations.

What Is A Visionary Leader?

Thoughts lead on to purposes; purposes go forth in action; actions form habits; habits decide character; and character fixes our destiny.

—Tryon Edwards

Visionary Leaders model the "standards" for organizational behavior, surround themselves with those who share espoused values, engage in participatory decision making and management, and give credit where credit is due, enabling employees to become peak performers. Lao-tzu's quote at the beginning of this chapter describes the empowerment employees feel when functioning in a positive and nurturing environment.

Most entrepreneurs, when asked to picture a company president, CEO, or Chairman of the Board, tend to visualize a rigid, highly-controlled person with a narrow outlook, who rules with an iron fist, goes strictly "by the book," takes few risks, and has little fun. This image represents the very antithesis of high-spirited entrepreneurs who give free rein to their enthusiasm and operate on intuition and "gut instincts."

Of course, somewhere between these two extremes a Visionary Leader can stand comfortably. That middle ground includes the following behaviors:

- *Living within identified values*
- *Thinking before acting*
- *Being consistent*
- *Communicating openly, honestly and directly*
- *Opening two-way lines of communication*
- *Exhibiting patience*
- *Creating purpose-driven environments*
- *Modeling professional behavior*
- *Understanding, appreciating and following established polices, procedures and systems*
- *Developing a participatory style of management and decision making*
- *Recruiting qualified employees*
- *Respecting diversity and the dignity of all human beings*
- *Valuing decisions made by others empowered to do so*
- *Striving to satisfy needs on Maslow's hierarchy*
- *Following the advice of President Theodore Roosevelt who observed:*

> The best executive is the one who has sense enough to pick good men to do what he wants done, and self-restraint enough to keep from meddling with them while they do it.

Onward and Upward

Like any change, graduating to the Visionary Leader phase can involve stress and tension. As the shift occurs, there may be in-fighting among departments, managers jealously guarding territories, and lingering mistrust of entrepreneurial motives. In the Visionary Leader phase, entrepreneurs must perpetuate the process of communication, cooperation and collaboration because one naturally leads to the next.

If entrepreneurs become proficient at the "Three Cs," they will remove most of the barriers to organizational growth and success. Entrepreneurs who learn how to effect change and are able to communicate this transformation to the organization will receive cooperation that results in collaboration which, in turn, makes the transition as painless as possible.

Organizations can create an environment where high levels of peak performance are a daily occurrence. Being a Visionary Leader is a constant growth process that continually redefines itself. Visionary Leaders consciously plan their actions and operate to achieve a continual win/win/win result. They test what they are doing to ensure it is in the best interest of all involved—customers, employees and the organization.

Visionary Leaders seek to discover what people are doing right. They rely on positive reinforcement to encourage the behaviors they desire from organizational members. They are consistent in their own behaviors and open, honest, and direct in their communication.

Visionary Leaders understand all behavior has consequences, and they use this knowledge to produce desired results. Their organizations are purpose-driven with each employee empowered to take responsible action to ensure the success of the enterprise. Empowering employees can mean discomfort and frustration as everyone adjusts to this new sense of responsibility. The transition period will be short if people feel they are truly moving away from pain toward pleasure.

Policies and procedures are recognized, valued and followed as the constitution of the business. Understanding the Vision and

Mission of the company allows everyone to work off the same page. Each person can concentrate on finding more effective ways to meet future challenges.

Visionary Leaders are both willing and able to satisfy the real needs of the organization. Their focus is on customer satisfaction with each person accountable to ensure that satisfaction. Quality and pride are evident, not just given lip service.

The organizations of Visionary Leaders provide meaning and a sense of significance. The company is an essential part of who organizational members are and intrinsic to the design of their lives, not just a place to go to make a living. Companies led by true Visionary Leaders offer the possibility of work environments that fulfill Maslow's Hierarchy of Needs and create wealth for everyone involved.

Differentiating Between Leadership and Management

Managers are people who do things right; Leaders are people who do the right thing.
—Warren G. Bennis

While entrepreneurs are skilled at creating business, competent managers are adept at ensuring appropriate policies, procedures and systems are in place to support the business over time. Good leadership and good management are both essential to the success of any business enterprise yet they do not share exactly the same character traits and qualities.

Endowed with inherent leadership capacities, entrepreneurs possess the inner strength, creativity, willingness to risk and love of a challenge coupled with the passion and commitment characteristic of natural leaders. Managers, on the other hand, are revered for many of the opposite qualities. Their roles require them to be cautious, weigh every decision, serve as liaisons between entrepreneurs and employees, and function as equalizers and gatekeepers.

Often managers manifest their creativity through their contributions to systems and procedures and in furthering the smooth operation of each department. Effective managers understand the organization's goals and objectives and possess the capabilities to help realize those goals and objectives.

Although entrepreneurs may have an innate ability to lead, they tend to believe they must manage the business as well. Their efforts to act as managers often cause them to behave erratically and conduct themselves in ways that are out of character for them.

Whenever entrepreneurs attempt to be something they are not, nor choose to be, things always get confusing. Developing an appropriate structure and implementing policies, procedures and systems in the entrepreneurial organization will do more to stabilize the organization and fulfill Maslow's needs than any managerial pretense on the part of the entrepreneur would or could produce.

The Visionary Leader developmental phase is differentiated from the three previous ones by:

- *Competent Leadership*
- *Consistent Behavior*
- *Effective Decision Making*
- *The "Three Cs": Communication, Cooperation and Collaboration.*

Competent Leadership

Trust, admiration and respect represent the foundation of competent leadership. Competence in leadership is best illustrated by looking at the ability of "leaders" to gain the trust, admiration and respect of their "followers."

When people trust the actions and motives of leaders and strive to emulate the examples they set, we can assume competence in leadership has been established. Great leadership is often described as the ability to consistently inspire ordinary people to do extraordinary deeds.

History has a way of defining the attributes of great leaders by focusing on "moments in time" that epitomize these historical figures—Lincoln's Gettysburg Address, Kennedy's Inaugural Address—"Ask not what your country can do for you but what you can do for your country"—and Martin Luther King's "I Have a Dream" speech.

Defining great leadership by these moments doesn't emphasize the true basis of leadership competency; that, of course, must be founded in consistency.

Consistent Behavior

Appropriately, consistent behavior is the cornerstone of the Visionary Leader phase. An aim of this fourth phase is to avoid prolonging the effects of ineffective behaviors demonstrated during Benevolent Dictator or Disassociated Director phases. This objective is accomplished by concentrating and capitalizing on the positive aspects of Entrepreneurial Genius behavior.

Trust, almost non-existent in the Benevolent Dictator and Disassociated Director phases, is the daily norm in this last phase because Visionary Leaders behave predictably, live within the identified company Values and understand how important their role is to the organization.

Predictability and consistency affect trust. When there is total trust, employees feel secure, valued and appreciated. Exhibiting consistent behavior frees entrepreneurs to lead the company by:

1. Compensating employees so they can fulfill their basic need for safety and security.

2. Providing a role model to emulate and nurturing a supportive "human" environment thus fulfilling the need for belonging.

3. Empowering employees with the authority, accountability and responsibility to achieve and gain competence to satisfy their esteem needs.

4. Allowing employees to participate in strategic planning, policy making, and corporate design to accommodate their need to know.

5. Establishing policies, procedures and systems to fulfill employees' needs for symmetry and order.

In order to behave consistently as Visionary Leaders, entrepreneurs need to understand and appreciate the reasons underlying their present behaviors. By realizing that certain behaviors result in predictable outcomes, they are then better equipped to accept accountability and responsibility to modify those behaviors that do not provide them with the outcomes they desire.

> *Everyone will experience the consequences of his own acts. If his acts are good, he'll get good consequences; if they're not, he'll suffer for it.*
>
> —Harry Browne

Motivating entrepreneurs to make the behavior modifications necessary to become Visionary Leaders usually involves a major paradigm shift in the entrepreneurial thought process. As behaviorist Maurice Massey suggests, the only time a substantial behavior change occurs is when a person has experienced a significant emotional event.

The distress of the Benevolent Dictator and Disassociated Director phases is often enough to cause entrepreneurs to affect this necessary shift—particularly during the Disassociated Director phase when pain and discomfort in the organization are the norm rather than the exception.

As Visionary Leaders set the tone in the organization, their behaviors act as the hub around which everything else revolves. If the hub is faulty, the wheels cannot perform regardless of how many spokes they have or how large their circumference. In business, if entrepreneurial behavior is inconsistent, the company cannot function effectively nor achieve its true potential. Entrepreneurs are clearly the center of influence for their organizations.

Effective Decision Making

> *Decision making is the specific executive task.*
>
> —Peter Drucker

A significant distinction between Visionary Leaders and Entrepreneurial Geniuses is the Visionary Leaders' ability to make effective decisions. Visionary Leaders consider and weigh the legal, moral and ethical concerns of all decisions and the potential long-term effects of them on the organization.

Freewheeling entrepreneurs tend to make spontaneous, emotionally-generated decisions in response to the moment. They are inclined to exhibit inconsistent behavior, often changing decisions as frequently as the wind shifts, leaving behind a trail of chaos in their wake.

When entrepreneurs have highly-developed decision making skills, they arrive at the best decisions possible based on the information available at the time. As decision making is an acquired skill, all of the components entrepreneurs and managers need for making effective decisions are present in the environment. Processing these components appropriately results in the most satisfactory decisions for all concerned.

Moreover, allowing employees to participate in the decision making process through open communication helps them to better appreciate where the organization is headed and why. Whenever information is exchanged, individual self-esteem is enhanced. By opening the lines of communication, entrepreneurs effectively send a message to employees that their input and perceptions are indeed valued.

The "Three Cs": Communication, Cooperation and Collaboration

When entrepreneurs behave as balanced Visionary Leaders, they and their organizations operate within the three most powerful and productive concepts of entrepreneurial and organizational transition: communication, cooperation and collaboration.

Communication, the first of the "Three Cs," must be in place to create an ideal corporate environment. Communication is based on how people interact and behave with one another. As behavior is the most obvious medium the entrepreneur uses to communicate with the organization, a lack of consistent behavior makes communication difficult, at best.

Effective communication leads to increased cooperation. Increased cooperation subsequently contributes to true collaboration. As these concepts are interrelated, one cannot be separated from the others. The "Three Cs" are critical in fulfilling employee higher needs—communication for enhancing esteem; cooperation for satisfying cognitive needs; and collaboration for fulfilling symmetry and order.

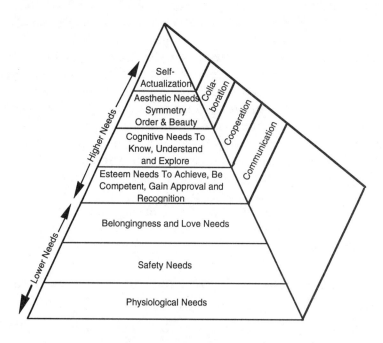

Maslow's Pyramid of Needs

The three components of entrepreneurial transitioning are shown at the appropriate higher levels. Communication is of paramount importance as everything is built upon it.

COMMUNICATION

To communicate, put your thoughts in order; give them a purpose; use them to persuade, to instruct, to discover. . . .
—William Safire

Effective, open communication must exist in any entrepreneurial organization or very little else will work. It is a vital tool in building and maintaining a business. Communication means sharing and exchanging information so messages are received and understood.

Effective communication often has little to do with the word choices themselves as much as with the manner and expression of their delivery. For this very reason, the adage that "actions speak louder than words" is truer than we would like to admit.

The ability to communicate effectively on a personal basis is a critical skill for entrepreneurs to develop.

The three components of communication are:

1. *Vocabulary—word choices.*

2. *Tone—voice inflection, speed, and pitch of delivery.*

3. *Body Language—subtle and obvious body movements and gestures accompanying delivery.*

Vocabulary

The first component, vocabulary, accounts for 7% of the message being communicated. Although there is value in carefully selecting words because they carry distinctions to help clarify the message, precision in language does not necessarily guarantee effective communication will result.

Tone

Tonality, on the other hand, accounts for 38% of the message to be communicated. Pitch, speed and intonation enhance the intended meaning of the words. If someone is enthusiastic when saying yes, listeners tend to believe they are in agreement with what others are expressing.

One common communication breakdown experienced in the small business world occurs when the entrepreneur and employees agree verbally to take action, yet employees sense the tentative tone of the entrepreneur's voice indicates a lack of commitment to implementing the decision.

Understanding the importance of tonality is critical for entrepreneurs. Using appropriate tone in the Entrepreneurial Genius phase created feelings of family and inclusion. Yet, in the Benevolent Dictator phase, tone produced tremendous pain. Still, in the Disassociated Director phase, the entrepreneur's tone suggested the organization was making excuses for not producing results.

It is very important in the Visionary Leader phase that tone be congruent with the intended message. The ability of entrepreneurs to say what they mean and mean what they say is definitely affected by the tone they use.

Body Language

Interestingly enough, body language accounts for 55% of the intent of the message being communicated. One reason for this percentage being significantly higher than the other two is the number of variations available in the way people use their bodies.

Bodies send silent messages through gestures and movements. One researcher estimated the human body can produce more than 700,000 physical postures to express any number of feelings and emotions.

Most of us rely on gestures to interpret another's intent. In business, observing one's behavior often reveals clues to the communicator's true feelings and, when coupled with their manner of speech, allows us to draw more in-depth conclusions. Many times this has proven to be more effective than relying on their actual words alone.

Developing an awareness of body language and learning to control it is an important aspect of entrepreneurial training. In a social context, people respond to cues whether or not those signals are expressed orally. The slightest change in expression and movement—the raise of an eyebrow, the tilt of the head—is noted, interpreted and evaluated according to a receiver's value system.

Why is it especially important for entrepreneurs to learn to control body language? What's the connection? The inconsistent behavior entrepreneurs frequently exhibit is a dead giveaway to observers.

GARFIELD reprinted by permission of USF, Inc.

Employees learn to be alert to entrepreneurial body language. Having experienced the irrational moods in earlier phases, particularly as Disassociated Directors, employees are suspicious of any changes. They will monitor the entrepreneur closely and critically, looking for any signal they are reverting back to their former inconsistent behaviors.

Communication is a Two-Way Street

Many entrepreneurs think communication is a one-way process—they issue "marching orders" for employees to carry out. As company founders and owners, entrepreneurs have become accustomed to this style of management. During the Entrepreneurial Genius phase, employees tolerate this method of communicating because the organization is casual and intimate.

In awe of the "brilliant" entrepreneur, employees willingly put up with unorthodox methods. They do not question the rationale of entrepreneurial directives. However, as the company expands and entrepreneurs exhibit Benevolent Dictator behaviors, casual one-way communication is no longer acceptable nor effective.

The dynamics of running the company have changed with the advent of many new departments and dozens of employees to communicate with. The systems may be open to a variety of interpretations. Thus, not only the informal method of communication but also the style of communicating must be altered to keep the company on track.

Two-way communication promotes trust and teamwork. It involves employees, eliciting their perspectives, viewpoints and feedback. This participation allows employees to satisfy esteem needs through recognition and approval as they contribute to the organization and the achievement of its goals.

Communication is Multi-Dimensional

Effective communication requires entrepreneurs to:

- *Exhibit more congruent behaviors*
- *Open lines of communication*
- *Hone listening skills*
- *Delegate authority along with appropriate accountabilities and responsibilities*
- *Model cooperation and teamwork*
- *Involve employees*
- *Make consistent decisions*

All of the above are components of effective communication. Some companies encourage open sharing through formal communication. They may conduct weekly status meetings or circulate information via memos and reports. Others use newsletters and informal types of communication such as tapping into the company "grapevine."

One advantage of the written word is that it represents tangible, physical evidence so employees know what is going on. Written documentation satisfies the need to know and understand. Without formal communication, employees feel isolated and upon hearing rumors, expect everything to fall apart. It is only natural and human nature to assume the worst in the absence of information.

In order to eliminate confusion and anxiety, it is the responsibility of entrepreneurs and senior executives to communicate with the organization in a timely manner. There are fewer surprises when employees understand exactly what is happening and why. Clarity helps in establishing high performance expectations.

If employees are uninformed and treated as if they don't belong in these discussions, they will behave as outsiders. Organizations benefit when employees are peak performers. For this reason, it is vital employees are at least informed of any organizational transitions and involved as much as possible. This responsibility falls squarely on the shoulders of Visionary Leaders to execute.

Communication Model as a Vehicle to High Performance

One entrepreneur in the Visionary Leader phase provided a model for a pending organizational change as follows:

Memo To All Employees

It has become necessary for us as a company to restructure ourselves. We would like everyone's input on this project. We plan to meet with all employees and make you a part of the process, asking for your opinions and sharing information.

We will begin by discussing our core values and determining what each of us cares about and believes in. Together, we are then going to articulate a compelling reason for this organization to exist into the future. We'll also define our immediate and long-term goals in the form of a Mission statement.

Subsequently, we will consolidate these ideas and develop a strategic plan. Before doing that, we will learn how to make decisions sharing the same process so that we are consistent within the organization. This process will give us the feedback we need to arrive at decisions we are all committed to implementing.

Through your involvement in the process, you will better understand the importance of your role in this organization, how it fits with those of others, appreciate what we value about you, and realize where the organization is ultimately headed.

Just by circulating this memo, the entrepreneur set an expectation for the organization and leadership. The memo was evidence of the intent to establish a new direction and create support for new policies, procedures and systems. By communicating the company's plans concerning what was about to happen, this entrepreneur was able to satisfy most employee needs. Everyone felt valued and important.

The entrepreneur's memo announced change was necessary and declared management was willing to listen and take action to ensure the future viability of the company while protecting employee interests. Systems would replace tradition. The memo communicated; it put everyone on notice they would share in formulating the new company structure. This subsequently resulted in more cooperation and greater collaboration within the organization.

Of course, once the memo was circulated, leadership was expected to deliver on these promises or the entire process would have broken down. Visionary Leaders must not only be willing to include the organization, they must follow through and make it a reality. Otherwise, their credibility will suffer more than if they just ignored everyone and made a unilateral decision on restructuring.

The need for change is usually an admission that "if we do what we've always done, we'll get the results we've always gotten." A repetition of past behavior will only recreate past results. By implementing the "Three Cs," the entrepreneur who wrote this memo made sure every employee was focused on developing a new way of operating and committing to its implementation.

COOPERATION

It is through cooperation, rather than conflict, that your greatest successes will be derived.

—Ralph Charell

Visionary Leaders appreciate how important cooperation is to realizing the organizational Vision. It is a prerequisite to collaboration and enhances communication.

Webster defines cooperation as "an association of persons working together for a common benefit." In business, cooperation is essential for organizational growth and development and critical to the success of entrepreneurs and organizational members. Cooperation is a joint effort; it calls everyone to action, working together for the mutual good.

When people form groups and band together, they increase their power. In this instance, "the whole truly becomes greater than the sum of the parts." Employees who feel empowered accomplish goals more effectively because they feel in control of their destinies. According to Jerry Aris, Chairman and CEO of Citizens Against Crime, Inc., the nation's largest seminar franchise company, this "multiplier effect" is the ultimate reason for all the successes of his company.

Cooperation is exemplified by teamwork and accomplishment of goals and objectives and leads to active involvement of employees in the management of the organization. This includes making decisions, creating strategic plans, establishing policies, procedures and systems, building organizational structure and contributing to other aspects of corporate development.

Teamwork does not mean following one person's lead or adhering to rigid guidelines. The concept of teamwork is a consensus of opinion within an organized structure whereby each team member has the opportunity to share in discussions and make decisions. When employees and entrepreneurs work collectively, trust levels naturally increase. During any cooperative stage of business, entrepreneurs are advised to monitor their behavior carefully for consistency as a team player for they set the example in the organization.

Structure

Creating a structure to support a service or purpose-driven organization is the goal of Visionary Leaders. This takes a strong commitment on the part of entrepreneurs in order to actualize the company of their dreams.

To lead the people, walk behind them.

—Lao-tzu

The traditional organizational chart places the entrepreneur at the top, senior executives next, with functions like manufacturing, marketing, sales and personnel at the bottom. Most conventional organizational charts, however, do not identify the accountability, authority and responsibility. If every person in the company has a place on the chart, they also need to know where they fit and how they contribute.

True Visionary Leaders *invert* the organizational chart, thereby moving themselves to the bottom. Akin to a construction project, inverting the chart places entrepreneurs at the base, enabling them to act as the cornerstone. Just like the base of a building, the foundation of an organization needs to be supportive and strong.

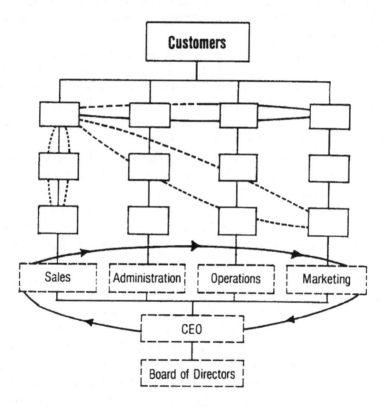

Visionary Leader Organizational Chart

The entrepreneur and the organization are structured to meet the needs of the employees and the customers have come back into focus.

This paradigm shift allows the entrepreneur to envision an organizational structure that serves the company. If the enterprise is to create support for everyone in the organization, the greatest pressure needs to be on those most capable of handling it— entrepreneurs and the board of directors. If these people are located at the bottom, they form the foundation for the structure.

Developing an inverted chart forces entrepreneurs to manage their companies based on a schematic of support. This inverted chart also includes all employees and specific responsibilities, accountabilities and authority of each. Such a structure ensures each person is connected to the ultimate goal of serving customers and maintaining company profitability.

While employees would undoubtedly welcome this inverted arrangement, entrepreneurs generally are skeptical at best. Even though they are non-conformists, they find it difficult to discard this particular business convention. This double-edged sword accounts for their strength and independence while diminishing those same characteristics in others.

Company structure, such as it is, in the Entrepreneurial Genius phase usually puts the customer first. With sales critical to achieving the goals of the organization, everyone focuses on keeping customers satisfied at any cost. As entrepreneurs evolve into Benevolent Dictators, the chart looks very different. Entrepreneurs appear at the top with the various levels of management listed beneath them. Benevolent Dictators are determined to make sure everyone knows exactly who is in charge.

Conspicuously absent is a place for the customer on this chart as evidenced by the concentration on internal activities. When entrepreneurs transition to the Disassociated Director phase and finally assign some accountability and responsibility, these changes are not usually reflected in the revised organizational chart. With everything in constant flux and entrepreneurs granting then rescinding accountability, the company is confusion-driven.

Some entrepreneurs would prefer no structure at all, and question its value to the organization. However, if they understand organizational structure as vital to effective management and the satisfaction of needs, entrepreneurs would more likely lay out a structure that allows some control yet frees them to support the entire company.

COLLABORATION

> *Coming together is a beginning,*
> *Keeping together is progress;*
> *Working together is success.*
>
> —Henry Ford

When the entrepreneur and the entrepreneurial organization communicate and cooperate, they are more apt to be focused on results and driven by purpose. If they share participatory, or collaborative, management and nurture a teaming environment, the likelihood that everyone will join forces, share information and work together is greatly enhanced.

If they know where they stand, employees have increased faith in the viability of the company and feel empowered. They become self-actualized as peak performers. If sales and operations are in balance, the wild pendulum swings cease. If each department and individual functions with the intent of delivering quality products and services to customers and potential customers, the result will be exactly that.

When communication, cooperation and collaboration are present within the organization, employees' needs are satisfied. Fulfilling these needs has a dual purpose in the entrepreneurial organization—employees achieve peak performance thus enabling entrepreneurs to realize their own personal missions and visions.

Acting the Role of a Visionary Leader

If you can't think your way to a new level of acting, you must act your way to a new level of thinking.

—Pascal

The philosopher Pascal theorized pretending to be someone by acting out their role makes it possible for people to become like that person. The only way to change behavior is to consciously act differently. If entrepreneurs cannot think themselves to a new level of acting, they must, then, act themselves to a new level of thinking. If they wish to become effective Visionary Leaders, they must act the part so well it becomes habitual and automatic.

Substance always follows style. If entrepreneurs style themselves after successful Visionary Leaders, they can actually model the characteristics of those Visionary Leaders. Entrepreneurs must understand their behavior has to be consistent with the perceptions people have about how leaders act. "By acting their way to a new level of thinking," they can become what they aspire to be.

People learn how to act in social situations by observing others and copying the reinforced behaviors. We employ the same technique as we learn to talk, walk, ride a bike, and dine out at a fine restaurant. The basic, socially-acceptable behaviors are copied from others when a child is between the ages of two and six years old. Others, in effect, provide the models.

Modeling the behaviors of Visionary Leaders is an important step in this process. Imitation is the sincerest form of flattery and occurs regularly in everyday life. People often imitate those they respect, believing if they follow their idols, they will be just like them. In businesses, employees often use this technique in an effort to advance their careers.

We are what we pretend to be, so we must be careful what we pretend to be.

—Kurt Vonnegut, Jr.

On the corporate ladder, people are led to believe particular titles require specific behaviors related to that title. For example, when employees observe the vice president behaving in a certain way, they may believe if they copy those behavioral characteristics, they will increase their chances of becoming a vice president.

They often assume the mannerisms of those they admire and, in the process of imitation, pattern their own behaviors after the ones they choose to emulate. In many corporations, people may dress similar to organizational leaders and assume their behaviors. John Malloy, author of *Dress for Success*, points out in his book that ambitious employees dress for the job they want, not the job they have, by using "power clothing" to elevate their status.

The Visionary Leader As a High Performance Athlete

Champion athletes in the performance of their sport are good examples of consistent behavior and the rewards that result from replicating effective action. When the chips are down, who do you give the ball to? Of course, you go to the player who consistently performs.

One NBA basketball star shoots 100 foul shots every day after practices, games and during the off season so when he is in that situation during a game, his behaviors will be automatic. He practices and consistently applies the same successful techniques each time so his actions become routine.

When this player is on the court and is fouled, his teammates have confidence in his ability to make the shot. This player is a peak performer. Peak performers by their very nature prepare; they do their homework to increase their competence and confidence. They know where they are going, how they're going to get there, and what to do when they arrive.

By the same token, Visionary Leaders who consistently model the behaviors they desire from the organization find those behaviors become habitual, automatic and trustworthy.

Past Performance As an Indicator of Future Behavior

"The best indicator of future behavior is past performance." The manner in which entrepreneurs handled past situations is a very good indicator of what employees can expect in the present. If entrepreneurs handled crisis situations poorly and produced less than acceptable results, employees come to expect this same pattern each time resulting in similar outcomes.

Employees who are conditioned to mistrust just about anything entrepreneurs do meet any shifts in behavior with skepticism. Employees have seen it all before. Being under the company microscope can present problems for entrepreneurs who don't realize they are always "on stage" even when they are in the process of rewriting their scripts.

Visionary Leaders understand this and prepare themselves and their organizations for what they want to achieve in the future. The entrepreneurial organization and the entrepreneur moving into the Visionary Leader phase must be ready to always look for what is right with the current transition rather than focusing on what went wrong in the past.

Making It Real

A frightened captain makes a frightened crew.

—Lister Sinclair

Entrepreneurs who appear uncertain of their actions will set off alarms in the organization. Employees expect leaders to be confident; they want leaders to inspire them.

When entrepreneurs present an attitude of self-confidence and model Visionary Leader behavior—the first step in internalizing these behaviors—employees may then be motivated to reach their full potential as top performers because Visionary Leaders are nurturing an environment of positive self-expectancy.

Rising to the Level of Expectation

There is no stimulus like that which comes from the consciousness of knowing that others believe in us.

—Orison Sweet Marden

During the Visionary Leader phase of development, a new level of expectation must arise. Expectation dictates results, and entrepreneurs must expect the best from themselves in order to expect the best from their employees.

Visionary Leaders must be willing and able to create a positive, productive working environment. They must also be willing and able to recognize and reward people for doing the right things. The role of nurturing must be shared by entrepreneurs and organizational members alike.

Creating a Positive, Nurturing Environment

It is easier to train employees when they have positive role models to imitate. For example, rewarding top employees with "Performer of the Week" recognition will do more to encourage peak performance in others than will hours of unbridled criticism.

Because they feel secure, peak performers are able to contribute more to a company than poor performers who often suffer from low self-esteem and are overly concerned with fulfilling their security and belonging needs.

Peak performers concentrate on solving problems rather than placing blame for them.

—Charles Garfield

Under-achievers can become more productive if their inner needs are recognized and nourished through positive reinforcement. In his book, *The One-Minute Manager,* Kenneth Blanchard relates the "Tale of a Whale" illustrating this point.

A whale can be trained to leap out of the water at any given moment even though its instincts tell it this can be fatal. Without going through the same training, the whale's baby will instantly copy the parent's behavior.

The whale's behavior is based on positive feedback: the whale is offered a special treat when it behaves as the trainer desires.

The process first includes a series of easily attainable skills for rewards. The level of difficulty increases to correspond to the natural steps in the learning process. As each step is accomplished, the level of difficulty increases as does the frequency of rewards. Only desired behaviors are rewarded.

As each skill is mastered, that mastery becomes the base line and then the norm, not the exception. Eventually, if the skill can be performed at the appropriate time, the corresponding reward will result.

Using a rope that is strung across the bottom of a pool, the whale must swim across the rope to receive its reward. Next, the rope is raised halfway to the surface. If the whale swims under the rope, no reward is offered by the trainer; if the whale swims over the rope, it is rewarded with a special treat.

Over a period of time, the rope is raised until it is above the surface of the pool, requiring the mammal to jump out of the water. This poses a dilemma for the whale, who instinctively wants to remain underwater.

Because of the encouragement it has received to this point, the whale is willing to jump out of the water; it knows there will be a positive outcome—its favorite fish as an acknowledgment of its feat. So going against its natural tendency, the whale takes the risk because it has been trained to expect only good results.

This training establishes a new level of performance by the whale. Akin to an organization attaining a new level of achievement, once the level has been established, it needs to be repeated consistently until it comes naturally.

When the whale's offspring comes along, it immediately begins copying the parent's behavior. No lengthy training process is necessary. The baby is able to perform the task of jumping over the rope in record time. The mother whale sets the example; her offspring learns by imitation. Thus, positive reinforcement almost always ensures a positive outcome.

One criteria for achieving the intended result is exemplified in Blanchard's tale. Entrepreneurs must understand the value of nurturing positive environments so the desired outcomes can be achieved.

Negative reinforcement, on the other hand, can be extremely destructive. B. F. Skinner demonstrated this theory by putting a pigeon into a maze and never giving it any positive reinforcement.

If the pigeon tried an incorrect path, it received negative feedback in the form of a small electrical shock. If the pigeon made a correct choice, no stimulus was given. Eventually, the pigeon ceased any attempt at finding the path to its reward, although it could both see and smell food. The pigeon preferred to die of starvation rather than risk making any choices.

Employees all too often hear about what they have done wrong or what didn't work. This emphasis on the negative coupled with a lack of positive stimuli even when they accomplish something good has the same effect on them as it had on the pigeon—they die.

Negative reinforcement rarely works well in a business context. In fact, it breeds dissatisfaction, disloyalty and even dishonesty. Kenneth Blanchard and Norman Vincent Peale noted in their book, *The Power of Ethical Management:*

> *People's negative feelings about their organization are at the root of unethical behavior.*

By utilizing varying degrees of positive reinforcement, Visionary Leaders can in essence assure their employees become peak performers and self-actualized, thus contributing significantly to the development of a highly successful enterprise.

Understanding What Motivates Others

David Yoho in his book, *Why People Buy Seminars*, suggests people change or are moved to act for one of four reasons:

- *Pride*
- *Gain*
- *Imitation*
- *Fear*

These four motivations also correlate to Maslow as follows:

1. Pride, as the specific motivation for people, coincides with the cognitive level of Maslow's hierarchy—the need to know, understand and explore. This motivator is the best and most powerful. Unfortunately, it is the least frequently used.

2. Gain is at the second highest level where positive reinforcement can help employees realize their dreams and satisfy a higher purpose for their lives. This corresponds to the level of esteem and the need to be competent, gain recognition and achieve.

3. Imitation, on Maslow's love and belonging level, is where role models help provide the incentive to perform well.

4. Fear, the most commonly used motivator, is at the lowest levels of Maslow's pyramid and can be most easily influenced through negative reinforcement.

Visionary Leaders who adapt their behaviors and use this information to create a positive, nurturing environment will produce the results they desire.

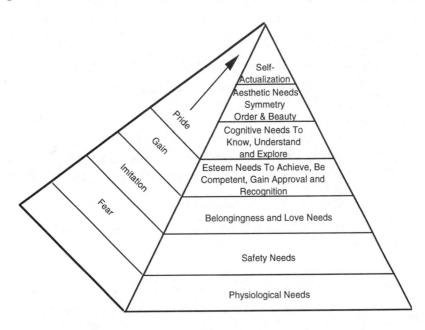

The four motivations and their comparison to Maslows's Pyramid of Needs

Teaming With the "Right" People

Savvy Visionary Leaders appreciate employees' desires to fulfill both basic and higher needs and willingly establish policies, procedures and systems to bring order out of the chaos. The resultant enthusiasm and teamwork usually increases both efficiency and effectiveness. Teamwork naturally leads to cooperation, where each "player" is functioning for the good of the organization.

Competent people who share common values should be in place to accomplish the corporate goals. If entrepreneurs and organizational members understand the implications at various levels in the growth cycles, they will be better prepared to anticipate and create an organization that doesn't have to go through immense pain to learn.

In the case of parents, the learning curve accelerates with the advent of the second and third offspring. The first child often provides a painful experience because parents are not prepared to handle their rearing.

By the time entrepreneurs have experienced the dilemmas and pain of the earlier phases of growth and development, they will modify their behavior and expectations more readily to enter the Visionary Leader phase.

Although their leadership abilities may be enhanced, their skills may still require development in order for them to be optimally effective.

Combining the Best of All Phases

It should be kept in mind that the Visionary Leader phase incorporates the best traits of each of the previous phases—the genius of Entrepreneurial Genius, the benevolence of the Benevolent Dictator and the director of Disassociated Director. Building upon and using the combination of all these positive traits contribute to becoming a Visionary Leader.

Chapter 4

Three-Dimensional Decision Making

Sometimes when I consider
What tremendous consequences
Come from little things . . .
I am tempted to think . . .
There are no little things.

—Bruce Barton

Decision making presents entrepreneurs with their greatest challenge, testing their true management abilities and leadership skills. Entrepreneurial decision making must become consistent and trustworthy if the organization is to ever reach its full potential.

The status of any enterprise is a direct result of the decisions and choices made by the entrepreneur and those who participate in the decision making process. The company audit, discussed in Chapter 5, is a vehicle for identifying the consequences of past decisions—and documenting the results for future reference.

A systematic and proven decision making process is crucial to entrepreneurs during any stage of their company growth. Strategic Planning, for example, is based on deciding what the organization needs to do in order to ensure long-term viability. Other more immediate management functions such as choosing between alternative types of systems, policies and procedures can only be defined via decision making.

Many entrepreneurs, known for their passion and enthusiasm, tend to reach decisions impulsively. Then, like many people, they justify their decisions with logic. Such decisions are often based solely on emotion and information immediately at hand rather than on intelligence gathered from a variety of diverse sources.

There is a substantial difference between intuition and emotion in the context of decision making. Intuition acts as an internal sensing device that can assist in making consistent decisions whereas emotion is rooted in the intensity of the moment. Often entrepreneurs allow transitory feelings to influence and overrule their better judgment.

Many individuals claim to have "gut level feelings" or "intuition" for things that, at times, are absolutely accurate. The trick to following gut reactions is determining when they are genuine, when they are wishful thinking, and when they are clouded by emotion. Most important is learning to distinguish the differences between them. Decisions made in the heat of the moment or as a result of mixed feelings are usually not the best possible decisions.

Entrepreneurs may be well-intentioned in making decisions in this manner, but they usually arrive at these decisions without considering any views other than their own. Effective decisions result in win/win/win scenarios. This means a variety of perspectives have to be accounted for and incorporated into the decision making process.

When entrepreneurs begin their businesses, quick decisions are often, of necessity, the order of the day. This style of decision making may serve fledgling companies and carry the organization to a certain point of development. During the Entrepreneurial

Genius phase, entrepreneurs are extremely adept at making intuitive decisions. Consequently, as the organization develops, confusion sets in as to what is intuitive and what has been colored by emotion or the complexity of the circumstances.

The question that arises is: "Why change now?" To a great extent, the entrepreneur has validated the existing decision making system and is comfortable with that process. Consequently, there is little rationale or justification for doing things any differently.

However, the lack of forethought in "it seemed like a good idea at the time" decision making is no longer advisable when there is so much more at risk. Poor decisions will have greater impact, be more difficult to rectify, and make the entrepreneur appear inconsistent, erratic, uninformed and unfocused.

As organizations grow, decisions have more far-reaching ramifications and widespread ripple effects. Greater resources, budgets, staff and planning demand a more careful and reasoned decision making process. Choices must now take into account a greater number of variables and diverse constituencies. If the enterprise is to be a long-term venture, neither emotion nor pure intuition can be the primary catalyst for choosing one alternative over another.

One important variable that Visionary Leaders carefully consider is how their decisions will affect employee needs. They understand how empowering it is for employees to be included in the decision making process. Visionary Leaders consistently ask two questions: "Is this decision within the Values?" and "Is this my decision to make?" Entrepreneurs who are willing to address both of these questions honestly will move their organization to increased levels of trust and performance.

Understanding how and why decisions are arrived at engenders employee trust that the choices being made accurately reflect their interests and concerns. If employees believe decisions are well thought out, working toward the implementation of the decisions and subsequent achievement of the desired outcomes is simplified. Consequently, employee trust in the decision making process becomes absolutely critical to long-term success.

Decision Making as an Acquired Skill

Management guru Peter Drucker believes decision making is the most crucial skill a business leader can acquire. The operative word in Drucker's statement is the word "acquire."

Even though human beings are born with the capacity to reason, decision making is an acquired skill, not just a random characteristic of mental processing abilities. The truth is, some people are more adept at developing their decision making skills, regardless of formal education and training.

The Decision Making Process Model discussed in this chapter represents a systematic Six Step approach interacting with Four Components. Through this process, individuals, teams and companies can more readily understand the important aspects of effective decision making and enhance their skills in this area.

As individuals, we are faced with a myriad of choices to make every day—from the most mundane matters of selecting what to wear and eat to the most intricate and involved commitments that may have a global effect. Yet, a great majority of people make decisions based on limited or faulty information without giving a second thought to the consequences that may result. They are often unconscious that the decisions they are making may significantly impact the quality of their lives or of others.

These decisions are often generated using unsophisticated decision making skills developed at an early age. As the need to make more effective decisions increases, the value of acquiring a reasoned and deliberate approach to decision making becomes essential. Consistently trying to build upon a skill foundation that is less than solid results in a skill base that is less than effective.

Anthony Robbins, author of *Unlimited Power* and *Awaken the Giant Within* , is credited with the following observation:

> *The quality of our life is directly proportional to the quality of our decisions.*

Three-Dimensional Decision Making

People make either one-, two- or three-dimensional decisions depending on circumstances. One-dimensional decisions take into account a single point of view, usually that of the decision maker. These decisions often contribute to the personal gain or benefit of the one individual making the decision.

On the other hand, two-dimensional decisions include the perspective of the decision maker and someone else. These decisions typically encompass the best interests of either one or, optimally, both parties involved.

Three-dimensional decision making—"win/win/win scenarios"—considers multiple viewpoints and alternatives before making a decision, predicting the effects on all concerned parties. These decisions attempt to embody the most desirable outcomes for the greatest number of people—customers, vendors, the organization, and entrepreneurs themselves.

Three-Dimensional Decision Making and Phases of Organizational Development

Entrepreneurial Geniuses primarily make three-dimensional decisions. Their style of management is participatory and frequently includes everyone in the decision making process. During this phase, the entrepreneur is focused on creating a sales-rich environment that nurtures the customer. Employees perform with a sense of pride and thus often perform at peak levels. The result is a natural win/win/win decision making scenario.

However, as the company is indeed sales-driven, Entrepreneurial Geniuses tend to ignore some of the critical operational decisions that may demand attention. By over-developing the business concept and under-developing the supporting corporate structure, these entrepreneurs tip the balance completely toward sales.

Eventually, as Benevolent Dictators arrive on the developmental scene, three-dimensional decision making disappears completely. During this phase, decisions are made by entrepreneurs behaving as "one-man shows," incorporating no perspective other than their own.

When the company swings away from being sales-driven and literally becomes operations-driven in focus, employees are the first casualties of this self-centered behavior. With Benevolent Dictators reluctant to delegate any decision making authority, employees feel like they are being treated as children. One of the motivations that helped them achieve peak performance— participation in decisions that affect them —quickly disappears.

Unfortunately, the more the Benevolent Dictators tighten their hold on the decision making reins, the less opportunity employees have to participate in the process. This lack of involvement adversely influences the collaboration that existed during the Entrepreneurial Genius phase and diminishes the order and symmetry of the work environment, keeping employees from fulfilling aesthetic needs.

Forced to descend a level on Maslow's pyramid under this Benevolent Dictatorship, employees then seek to satisfy cognitive needs. Unfortunately, with entrepreneurs keeping their own counsel and confiding in no one, the employees' need to know, understand and explore also suffers.

Continuing the descent, employees seek next to satisfy their esteem needs. However, because Benevolent Dictators handle everything and refuse to allow participation, employees' attempts to gain approval and recognition prove futile. Individual self-esteem is at its lowest.

With the higher levels of needs stripped away, employees are forced to seek belonging and love. Here again, Benevolent Dictators deprive employees of ways to meet these needs. This behavior continues to distance the entrepreneur from the workforce. Employees cannot feel part of an organization they are denied participation in.

When you cease to make a contribution, you begin to die.
—Eleanor Roosevelt

When entrepreneurs become Disassociated Directors, they tend to base their decisions solely on momentary "snapshots" of the organization. With the company swinging wildly from a sales to an operations focus and back again, conditions rarely improve for employees, and entrepreneurs grow more and more frustrated.

Truly confusion-driven and consistently inconsistent, Disassociated Directors either constantly reverse their own decisions or those made by others or refuse to make any decisions at all. Disassociated Directors do not trust any decisions made and are compulsive about changing them.

Look, just forget what I said about quick fixes and easy solutions and come up with a quick fix or an easy solution.

William Hamilton's cartoon is reprinted by permission of
Chronicle Features, San Francisco, California.

A Hypothetical Case Study

A Disassociated Director we will refer to as Bob, decided his company needed a new telephone system. Bob had understandable but emotionally-oriented reasons for making this decision. Once, while Bob was on the factory floor, he was unable to respond to an incoming call. As a result, he experienced the momentary frustration of not being able to quickly access a telephone.

Given that none of his line workers needed to use a telephone in accomplishing their tasks, extensions had never been installed on the factory floor. In fact, access to a telephone on the shop floor would have been distracting.

On another occasion, Bob could not access an outside line because all the existing lines were busy—again, frustration. He also began to dislike the bulky design of the telephones—another emotional reaction. However, one of Bob's most defensible reasons for wanting a new telephone system was the indication the company was on the verge of explosive growth.

Considering all these factors at face value, Bob decided to buy a new telephone system, justifying rather than evaluating the real need. Bob believed the company required telephone accessibility everywhere and installed a system with the capacity to "grow" and accommodate up to 5,000 extensions. Additionally, he ordered 40 innovative, high-tech handsets complete with a computerized switching capacity.

The new system was subsequently installed at a cost in excess of $60,000. Bob, of course, got "a good deal" as the salesman whom he met on an airplane showed him the lease payments were less than what a full-time receptionist would earn if compensation and benefits were taken into account.

The salesman succeeded in convincing Bob he would make that amount up easily by effectively handling just one important phone call. The fact the organization had fewer than 30 employees, only several of which needed any telephone access to accomplish their job tasks, seemed to escape Bob's consideration.

Bob defended this emotional decision with "logic" that sounded something like: "I want telephone access wherever I am in the factory. As we're going to grow much bigger, we can also cross train factory workers to handle overflow calls on occasion." These reasons seemed like a good idea at the time because the company was indeed experiencing phenomenal growth. No one could argue telephone accessibility throughout the plant was not a sound idea.

When Bob immediately purchased the biggest and best telephone system he could find, what resulted was an excessive and expensive system requiring monthly payments that far exceeded the company's current financial resources.

Did Bob really need all this equipment? Were other options available to him? Did he really have all the appropriate information he needed to make this decision? Bob made a decision based on the old methods he had always used, or maybe no method at all. Had an effective decision making process been in place, Bob might have made a different (wiser) decision.

Applying the Decision Making Process Model

Out of intense complexities intense simplicities emerge.
                              —Sir Winston Churchill

The Decision Making Process Model that follows represents a systematic approach designed to organize the components and variables involved in reaching the best possible decisions. This process helps entrepreneurs and their organizations make decision making as simple, straight-forward, consistent and effective as possible.

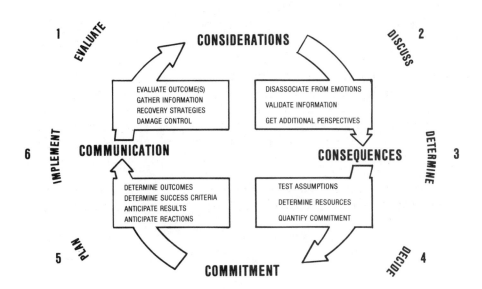

The Decision Making Process Model consists of Four Components, designed to interact with Six specific Steps. Process Points throughout the steps require attention for the model to be effective. Three initial questions provide individuals and organizations with a common ground or point of reference from which to begin the decision making process.

Adhering to the Decision Making Process Model ensures the organization communicates, cooperates and collaborates—the "Three Cs" of an effective entrepreneurial organization.

Three initial questions regarding a decision are always:

1. *Is this decision within the Values?*

2. *Is this decision legal, moral and ethical?*

3. *Is this **my** decision to make?*

Decision makers must also keep in mind the following concepts:

- *Decisions are made on emotion then defended by logic*

- *Evaluate the outcomes; do not justify the decision*

Four Major Components

The four major components of the process model that facilitate effective decision making are:

1. *Considerations*

2. *Consequences*

3. *Commitment*

4. *Communication*

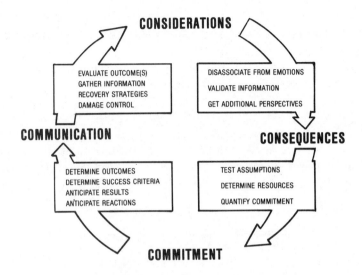

Considerations

Most people would rush ahead and implement a solution before they know what the problem is.

—Q.T. Wiles

This component includes evaluation of variables and analysis of options applied to both past and future decisions. Visionary Leaders and peak performers recognize that more than one option or alternative exists, each with its own set of considerations to evaluate.

Consequences

Logical consequences are the scarecrows of fools and the beacons of wise men.

—Thomas Henry Huxley

Research conducted during development of this model indicated the Consequences component is by far the most crucial one for entrepreneurs to grasp and internalize. In determining Consequences for each potential alternative, entrepreneurs and decision makers must perceive the need for prudent choices, remembering Newton's law that "for every action, there is an equal and opposite reaction."

GARFIELD reprinted by permission of USF, Inc.

Recognizing that each course of action discussed can and will create future successes and potential failures for the organization and its employees, entrepreneurs develop a new level of appreciation for the need to improve their skills in decision making.

Commitment

Take time to deliberate; but when the time for action arrives, stop thinking and go in.

—Andrew Jackson

The Commitment component helps the organization and the entrepreneur discover the resources needed for successfully implementing the action plan. In deciding what course of action to take, the organization is tactically committing the necessary resources to accomplish the identified outcomes.

Whenever a decision is made, it is important to understand the commitment involved in deciding and implementing a particular course of action. Quantifying the commitment that the entrepreneur and the organization are willing to make to a specific decision creates an opportunity to conduct a "reality check." If the entrepreneur is 100% committed and the organization is only 50% committed, then some additional discussion must take place.

The commitment an entrepreneur and the organization have to a course of action must also be balanced against the other priorities the organization is currently pursuing.

Communication

Simply stated, involving the right people at the right time in the decision process.

—Wayne Barlow

Once a decision has been reached and the courses of action outlined, communication becomes the primary component to ensure success. Communication addresses how the appropriate people receive specific information in a timely way so as to achieve the intended or desired results.

This includes a follow-up assessment to track what is really happening and to determine if the identified outcomes are being achieved. By continually monitoring progress, needed course corrections are indicated.

The Six Steps of Effective Decision Making

Steps to be taken sequentially during the process are:

1. *Evaluate - Outcomes of past actions*
2. *Discuss - Alternative courses of action*
3. *Determine - Consequences of each action*
4. *Decide - What specific action to take*
5. *Plan - How the action will occur*
6. *Implement - The course of action*

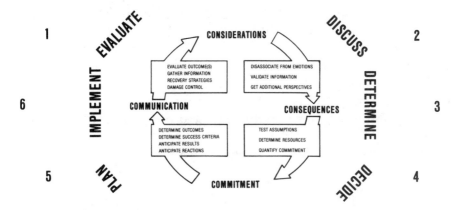

Data >Information > Knowledge > Intelligence

Understanding the distinctions between these concepts and having sources or conduits in place for intelligence gathering can enhance the quality of the decision making process and the outcomes.

Data is disorganized information, or, information is simply data that has been organized. Knowledge involves selecting and assimilating particularly relevant information to make a particular decision. Intelligence requires knowing what to do with the knowledge, subsequently empowering the decision makers with a more effective means for creating the results they desire.

Well-developed intelligence gathering can prepare decision makers to appreciate the myriad of options and alternatives available to them. The quality of the decision is always better when a variety of options and contingencies have been considered.

"Intelligent" means a person who can see implications and draw conclusions.

—Babylonian Talmud, Hagiga

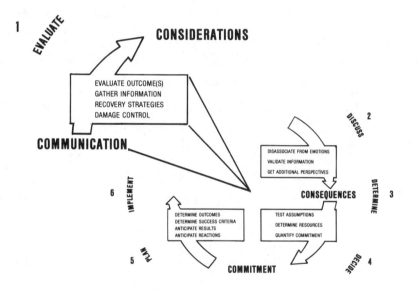

Step 1—Evaluate

Initially, the Evaluate Step is utilized to study past choices. At the end of the process—after Step 6—the decision maker comes full circle and returns to Step 1 to assess the outcomes of the decision just chosen and implemented. Evaluate, therefore, can be viewed as both the beginning step and final step, as each course of action will set in motion opportunities for new and different decisions.

Process Points in this step include:

- *Evaluate Outcomes*
- *Gather Information*
- *Recovery Strategies*
- *Damage Control*

Evaluate Outcomes

In every enterprise consider where you would come out.
—Publilius Syrus

Evaluating Outcomes refers to the assessment of results obtained from previously implemented ideas. As current decisions are directly impacted by past choices, it is important to evaluate how the outcomes of prior decisions impact the current one. Questions that can be helpful in evaluating outcomes include:

- *What were the results of the previous decisions?*
- *Were those the desired results?*
- *If not, why not?*

A benefit of consistently evaluating outcomes is knowing that future decisions will also undergo scrutiny. This understanding contributes positively to the quality of thinking that goes into the next set of choices.

An evaluation process forces those making the decision to step back and take sufficient time to anticipate the type of outcomes their decision ultimately will have. This cognitive awareness of the impact of decisions in and of itself improves overall decision making skills.

Gather Information

Information may be accumulated in files, but it must be retrieved to be of use in decision making.
—Kenneth J. Arrow

This involves the collection and processing of all information influencing or affecting the outcomes of past or future decisions. Questions requiring answers include:

- *Did we have data, information, knowledge or intelligence?*
- *How credible were our sources?*

- *Was the information fact or opinion?*
- *What has been our evidence procedure in the past for determining successes or failures?*

Recovery Strategies

It is a bad plan that admits of no modification.

—Publilius Syrus

At times, results are less than complete. For instance, sales may have increased, but less then anticipated. Considering this aspect prior to making the decision helps in understanding what has to be done next. Developing recovery strategies well in advance of any breakdowns facilitates the ease of responding in a timely way. In new decisions recovery strategies are commonly referred to as contingencies. Sample questions include:

- *What kind of recovery, if any, might we have to make?*
- *Do we have the resources to make the recovery?*

After making a decision, it is very important to monitor and manage the outcomes of that decision. By periodically taking a pulse of what is happening, it is easy to make an accurate assessment of possible course corrections required to adequately meet the stated objectives.

Damage Control

In every affair consider what precedes and what follows, and then undertake it.

—Epictetus

Damage control requires an understanding of what needs to be done to salvage a situation and how quickly it needs to be accomplished. This, of course, sets in motion an entire series of new decisions to be made.

It also questions whether the damage can be contained and, if so, what else will this "disaster" affect. It explores existing contingency plans and examines whether they will be effective in ultimately bringing about the desired outcomes.

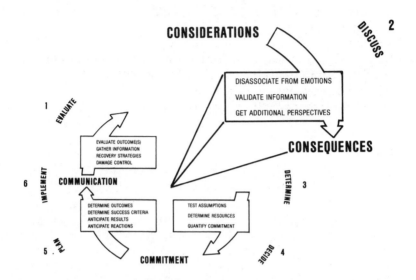

Step 2—Discuss

At this point in the process, decision makers identify and discuss all the considerations and options available. Discuss available alternatives with those who possess and can contribute expertise. Ivory tower discussions are dangerous to long-term growth.

Process Points in this step include:

- *Disassociate from Emotions*
- *Validate Information*
- *Get Additional Perspectives*

Disassociate from Emotions

The timid are easily drawn into hazardous resolutions by despair, as are the rash by recklessness.
—Francesco Guicciardini

Emotions can cloud issues and adversely impact decision making. Detaching oneself from personal feelings and approaching a decision from a disassociated point of view enables those making the decision to achieve more clarity and expand their perspectives.

Visionary Leaders tend to make their best decisions from a physiological state often described as one of calm confidence. This state is also commonly referred to as "being centered."

When entrepreneurs understand and feel comfortable with being more objective, they are less likely to make "erratic" decisions.

Validate Information

If you get all the facts, your judgment can be right; if you do not get all the facts, it can't be right.

—Bernard Baruch

Ensuring the accuracy of the input is critical and requires attention to detail and constant checking and rechecking. The adage "garbage in = garbage out" is important to keep in mind. Many times decisions are made and "marching orders" given only to discover later that the decision utilized faulty information, and perhaps no real need existed. Questions that can be helpful include:

- *Does the information reflect merely a single or multiple views?*
- *Is it opinion, hearsay or fact?*
- *How do we know?*
- *Are there measurable statistics and surveys to support it?*

Get Additional Perspectives

Teams are less likely [than individuals] to overlook key issues and problems or take the wrong actions.

—Eugene Raudsepp

Using every means available to uncover diverse and expert points of view needed to make the best possible decision will provide a significant return.

Effective decision makers interview customers, vendors, employees, and anyone else who may be affected by a decision. Increasing the contributing resources and examining the choices

three-dimensionally ultimately surfaces the most feasible courses
of action to be implemented.

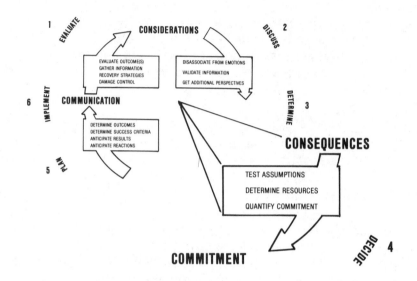

Step 3—Determine

In this step, the consequences of the alternatives being
discussed and contemplated are determined. Each alternative or
option carries with it specific consequences that must be explored
and understood prior to deciding on what action to take.

Step 4—Decide

When consensus to move forward is reached, and a course of
action decided upon, it is time to assess the feasibility of the choice
and the level of commitment people have to implementation of
this specific option.

Process Points in this Step include:

- *Test Assumptions*
- *Determine Resources*
- *Quantify Commitment*

Test Assumptions

He thinks not well, that thinks not again.

—George Herbert

Decision makers often create "hypothetical scenarios" to help them understand the implications of their choice. It is during this "what if?" exercise that the assumptions pertaining to this choice are challenged for their accuracy and validity.

Determine Resources

A good way to outline a strategy is to ask yourself: "How and where am I going to commit my resources?" Your answer constitutes your strategy.

—R. Henry Miglione

Identifying resources needed to execute this course of action helps in determining the potential success of implementation. If an idea is worth pursuing, the required resources must also be available.

Allocating resources is an exercise that helps decision makers realize the commitment of money, time and people necessary to successfully accomplish the objective. Additionally, the level of priority this course of action commands will help determine the appropriate resources and establishing time frames for accomplishment. Questions that can help clarify the magnitude of a particular undertaking might include:

- *Do we need more raw materials, a larger staff, working capital?*

- *What are the existing commitments of the resources and the possible consequences we may suffer if the implementation fails?*

- *What happens to other priorities while we focus our attention on achieving this one?*

Some decisions are practically "no brainers" with little or no resource allocation required for effective implementation. Others are less obvious, and people may not naturally understand what it will take to ensure success. In this instance, total clarity is critical to achieving the intended outcomes.

Quantify Commitment

It is useless to make formal decisions with which group members informally disagree.

—William G. Dyer

This means giving those in the decision making process a true reality check about the belief they have regarding the decision individually and collectively. It also helps in establishing the level of priority being given to this course of action. Unless those involved in achieving the results of a decision are engaged in making it, loyalty or commitment to the implementation of that decision is unlikely. Quantifying commitment means asking questions such as:

- *What are the odds the decision will be carried through?*

- *Is there total commitment to this decision or only 75%?*

- *If people are ambivalent, does this mean the decision is not considered a top priority or does it mean it is unpopular and lacks support?*

Not all decisions merit 100% endorsement, so quantifying the commitment serves as an orderly way of grading and prioritizing those decisions that must be made and implemented in a timely manner. An equation useful in determining the anticipated success of a decision is as follows:

1. *Assign a score to the quality of the idea The scale is 1-10, with 10 being the best idea.* **This is the Idea Score (IS).**

2. *Assign another score to the abilities of the organization given its priorities and resources (money, time, people).The scale is 1-10, with 10 being the best ability.* **This is the Implementation Strategy Score (ISS).**

3. *Multiply the IS by the ISS to arrive at a Success Score (SS).*

$$IS \; x \; ISS = SS$$

An example of this equation might look as follows:

IS = 5 (It is a good idea but not a great one)
ISS = 8 (Implementation appears quite feasible)

$$
\begin{array}{r}
5 \\
\underline{x\,8} \\
40
\end{array}
$$

An alternative option may score as follows:

IS = 10 (A great idea—everybody loves it)
ISS = 3 (Feasibility of implementation seems remote)

$$
\begin{array}{r}
10 \\
\underline{x\,3} \\
30
\end{array}
$$

In many cases, an average idea that has a fairly strong chance of being implemented would be a more desirable alternative than a great idea that is going to be difficult or costly to actualize. Quantifying the level of commitment to a given idea aids in determining whether the intended outcomes are indeed achievable.

Each organization must determine how high a Success Score needs to be to implement a decision. In some organizations, a score of 50 is good enough to undertake a project. In others, if financial risk needs to be minimized or security needs are high, a much higher score may be required.

The organization can decide to "re-prioritize" the decision and allocate sufficient resources to take an ISS of "3" and convert it into a "10"; however, that decision must be processed and undergo the same scrutiny as the initial one. Scores influenced by emotion have a tendency to net unrealistic results.

Realizing we exist in a fluid and dynamic environment, the organization must appreciate the "realistic" uses of resources and the limits of its capacities.

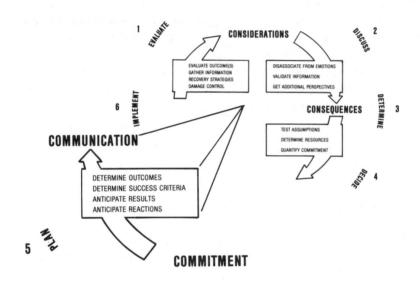

Step 5—Plan

By this stage of the process, there should be agreement to take specific action. Creating a plan for implementing the decision is crucial to the success of the course of action chosen.

Process Points useful during this step include:

- *Determine Outcomes*
- *Determine Success Criteria*
- *Anticipate Results*
- *Anticipate Reactions*

Determine Outcomes

If our original plan had a lower goal, we would have achieved less.

—William E. Foster

In order to plan effectively, intended results have to be identified or determined. A general idea of the desired results was generated during Step 1 when we evaluated previous outcomes. In this phase, we are now concerned with identifying the specific and expected outcomes for this course of action.

Understanding what specific results the decisions are intended to have and how the organization will achieve each is critical to both short- and long-term decision making.

It should be possible to predict outcomes with a fair amount of accuracy because they have to be measurable. Into this equation, we add the success criteria established next.

Determine Success Criteria

Productivity is only productivity if it's measurable.

—Anonymous

Establishing a measurement standard provides a means against which the results of the decision can be assessed and evaluated instead of justified. Success Criteria can be measured with questions such as:

- *How are we going to measure the effects of decisions and courses of action?*
- *How will we know if we are successful?*
- *Is a 35% increase in sales considered acceptable?*
- *Will reaching two-thirds of the goals be deemed a failure?*

Knowing the intended outcome allows the organization to measure that outcome. It is not enough to establish success criteria if no one is accountable for its measurement.

Anticipate Results

Good results without good planning come from good luck, not good management.

—David Jaquith

If the decision is outrageously successful and product demand goes through the roof, the organization must be in a position to keep up with delivery. Decision makers need to consider:

- *If these goals are achieved, how will that affect decisions in process or other plans on the drawing board?*
- *Will additional staff be hired or new equipment purchased?*
- *How will the results affect future growth?*
- *What will we do about B if C comes through first?*
- *What don't we have in place that we will have to put in place immediately?*

By asking questions such as these, the organization can gain a better perspective of the ripple effects they will experience if the intended results do occur.

Anticipate Reactions

It's in changing the way people work that...the answers to productivity are going to be found.

—John Sculley

Being prepared to handle the reactions of customers, employees and others is critical in making the best decisions possible. If an internal decision is unanimously supported by the staff yet 80% of the customers do not value it, the risks of proceeding have to be weighed. Of course, this would not happen if those customers were involved earlier in the process.

This requires asking:

- *How will the staff, customers and vendors feel about this decision?*
- *Is there criticism of the plans?*
- *Does data exist to sufficiently explain the decision to and satisfy concerns of staff, customers or vendors?*

Some employees may be adamantly opposed to any new ideas; others may only need a minimum of convincing before they come aboard. Knowing the internal sales process for new ideas is helpful in ensuring support is available for the intended course of action.

If an employee, vendor or key customer is "known" to react with certain patterns of behavior, decision makers must be proactive to ensure success rather than forced to be reactive.

Step 6—Implement

When the decision has been made and everyone has declared commitment to the "plan," it is time to act on the decision. Implementing a decision or course of action means getting the appropriate information to the appropriate people at the appropriate times in order to attain the desired outcome. Ideally, there is communication, cooperation and collaboration. This brings us back full circle to Step 1.

Putting the Process into Practice

Now the organization has implemented a deliberate process for making decisions, we can return to our hypothetical case study of Bob and his telephone system. Since our last encounter with Bob, he has become a Visionary Leader and acquired effective decision making skills.

He now approaches the purchase of a new telephone system by systematically going through the Decision Making Process with his organizational members. Using the model, Bob and his employees begin gathering the information needed to make an evaluation:

- *Do we honestly need a new phone system?*
- *Who must have an extension and why?*

During the information gathering process, they discover only 12 of the 27 employees regularly need access to a telephone in order to accomplish their typical daily tasks. They also find there are others who need only periodic access, which is currently available in the employee lounge.

In checking with customers and vendors, however, Bob and employees learn these important people often encounter a busy signal when they try to contact the company. This research suggests at least one good reason exists for increasing the number of incoming telephone lines.

Everyone is in agreement that Bob needs to have access to a telephone as he moves about the different parts of the factory which has expanded from 5,000 to 40,000 square feet. Bob shouldn't have to walk all over the place in an effort to respond quickly to an important call.

Putting his personal preferences aside, Bob makes sure he disassociates himself from his emotions. He realizes that even though he wants a new telephone system, he may only need a private line in addition to his extension on the company switchboard.

He also accepts the fact he may be the only one who dislikes the current telephone enough to justify a model that is less bulky and fits his hand better. Through this process, Bob finds out he can purchase a cordless telephone he can carry and use throughout the factory.

Consequently, Bob is ready to discuss and determine the consequences of the decision:

- *How much will the phone system cost?*
- *Will everyone be satisfied with it?*

He and his staff test assumptions they have come up with and find they have forgotten to include the night watchman in the process. They conclude that he, too, should have a portable telephone as he makes his rounds so he is accessible at all times.

This additional phone will add to the cost of the new system, so when determining the resources needed, Bob will have to adjust his cash flow allocation—another consequence requiring consideration and discussion.

When it comes to quantifying commitment, everyone agrees the revised decision regarding the purchase of a new telephone system is sound and supports the investment in upgrading some telephones and adding additional incoming lines.

Having considered all the factors involved, Visionary Leader Bob and his employees determine that the outcomes from this decision appear to be positive ones. Customers and vendors will be able to contact the company with little frustration and no busy signals; salesmen will have dedicated lines for their work; Bob has a telephone at his fingertips; and the cost is only a fraction of the $60,000 originally estimated.

The organization decides one of their success criteria will be met if customers can reach the company on their first attempt to call. Another success criteria would be if Bob is satisfied with his new model and is able to use the phone anywhere in the factory.

Throughout the process, Bob and his organization continue to communicate, cooperate and collaborate as they move through the various aspects of the decision making process together. This ensures each is able to satisfy their highest inner needs by their involvement in the process.

While it is important for employees to understand how decisions are reached, it may not be necessary for the entire organization to participate in the decision making process every time. However, employees must be able to believe and trust that the decisions that are made will reflect their interests and concerns.

This flexible decision making process can be used in all stages of entrepreneurial growth. Although it may not always be necessary to take the decision through all phases, it is important the skills be built on a consistent and disciplined approach to the process.

The organizational use of this decision making process will give everyone a common "point of departure" and assist in the communication process which ultimately contributes to real collaboration.

Decision making should be an on-going process, not an isolated event. By using the Decision Making Process Model, you will base your decisions from the context of a consistent framework.

Chapter 5

Conducting the Organizational Audit:
Time for a Reality Check

Understanding where you are and how you got there is the only
way to decide where you are going....
—Unknown

The Organizational Reality Check or Audit, is a discovery tool used to determine where the entrepreneurial organization stands in its development. The audit indicates specifically what the organization currently does, and what the current processes and work flows are for accomplishing its tasks.

Focusing on major areas such as operations, sales and marketing, finance and administration, the Reality Check pinpoints the status of the entrepreneur's venture. It forces the organization to take a good look in the mirror and confront what is reflected there. The Reality Check can assist in pointing out where there may be gaps.

The Reality Check allows entrepreneurs and their employees a forum from which to begin a new level of open, honest, and direct communication, enhancing cooperation and ultimately leading to collaboration.

The audit examines the present and the past, revealing where the organization is, whether goals have been achieved and what circumstances led to the current reality. Yet, it is also the key to the future.

Conducting the Reality Check enhances planning for the future. Armed with accurate audit information, the entrepreneur and the organization are then able to make decisions on critical short-term (tactical) and long-term (strategic) issues.

> *The ultimate security is your understanding of reality.*
> —H. Stanley Judd

The audit shows who has the current authority, accountability and responsibility for different tasks and functions and reveals the existing organizational structure. It may also expose facts and information within the organization that were little known, even to the entrepreneur.

The organizational audit does more than just look at structure. It also looks at the individuals within the company, including the entrepreneur. To be effective as Visionary Leaders, entrepreneurs must know how they are perceived by the organization and how their actions are being interpreted internally and externally. Is the entrepreneur contributing to a positive, safe, and secure organizational environment or inhibiting the ability of the staff to take action?

Do organizational members have direction? Are they serving customers well? Is the company maintaining the delicate equilibrium to be a service-driven organization or is it out of balance? Do all activities reflect the Values of the entire organization and do they lead to specific goals? Has the organization set and achieved realistic goals?

Another function of the organizational audit is assessing the competition. The Competitive Analysis section in Sales and Marketing will evaluate the organization's place within the industry. Comparisons can then be made as to how it measures up to the competition in areas such as: compensation, benefits, revenues, profitability, and customer satisfaction.

Recognizing that each function and task within the organization should have led to a specific result, ideally contributing to specific goals, the entrepreneur can now learn how and why the company has arrived at its present point of development.

While conducting the Reality Check, it will serve little purpose to distribute praise or assign blame for the organization's status. The company simply is where it is. Discovering the reasons, right or wrong, will be helpful in devising strategies and tactics to move forward, but in most cases, enough time and energy has been spent in finger pointing. Conducting the Reality Check poses a special challenge to the entrepreneur and the organizational members because everyone must be careful to keep emotions to a minimum.

> *If we open a quarrel between the past and the present, we*
> *shall find we have lost the future.*
>
> —Sir Winston Churchill

Focusing on what worked and what didn't work in the past can be used to capitalize on what could happen from now on. It should not surprise anyone to learn that communication breakdowns contributed significantly to any unattained goals that are identified, as communication is paramount for success, and conspicuously absent in failure.

Utilizing the Reality Check

Most entrepreneurial organizations will already have established basic traditional departments such as sales and marketing, customer service, operations, administration, and accounting. However, in many instances, the functions of the individuals within those departments may or may not actually be consistent with their position, responsibilities or understanding of co-workers and customers. This can and often does cause confusion both internally and externally.

For example, at one company undertaking a Reality Check, five staff members in the Sales department were asked to describe the accountabilities and responsibilities of employees in a customer service situation. A wide spectrum of responses followed. A specific question revolved around Customer Services' role in the overall sales and marketing strategy.

The entrepreneur and the vice president of Customer Service disagreed on the priorities of that department. The vice president viewed the department as a support sector— giving advice, fielding complaints, troubleshooting. As a result, employees were instructed to answer only those questions directly related to the customer's specific problem.

The entrepreneur, on the other hand, viewed Customer Service as a prime sales function, insisting that the best time to sell additional products was while servicing an existing customer. When the Reality Check uncovered the efficiency, but ineffectiveness, of the vice president's system, a tactical change was made, not only to answer customer questions and complaints, but also to make suggestions and field questions about new products.

Customer Service employees were empowered to solve problems first and then ask questions to determine if the customer needed different or additional products. Just by following these guidelines, the company experienced over a 100% increase in orders within the next 90-day period.

Obviously, changes in training and compensation as well as job performance criteria were involved in the transition. The organization flourished once all the players understood the purpose of their department and how it contributed to the organization's success.

Customer satisfaction scores also soared because customers discovered the organization actually did care about and want their business.

Gathering Input

Input to the audit should be elicited from the entrepreneur, employees, customers and vendors. If the real reason entrepreneurs are in business is to service customers, then it would seem reasonable to talk with everyone involved to discover realities, incorporate specific ideas, gain new insights and begin the communication, cooperation and collaboration process.

The audit can also prove insightful regarding the administration of employee benefits such as vacations and sick leave. Through the audit process, entrepreneurs often come to realize that they have no established guidelines, rather, that each request is handled as an exception or on a personal basis.

Through the audit process, entrepreneurs become aware of which policies they have and which they lack, and develop an understanding of how important those policies are to establishing consistency and fulfilling employee needs. Moreover, they realize that they must establish policies *at the same time* they implement future strategies—not after the fact.

Awareness of Work Flow

The interrelationships of work flow and communication between departments are often assumed to be understood. More often than not, there exist significant differences between "the perceptions" and "the reality" of how departments relate and how work flows occur. A true understanding must be established. The audit acts as a tool for this discovery.

A chart of the work flow process is an excellent visual aid to help the organization understand its current processes and systems, how they interrelate, and what happens as a result. In many instances entrepreneurial organizations find that employees aren't sure what happens in other departments, and in low-trust organizations do not care.

The Process

The following section offers a series of questions with which to begin the Organizational Audit. The Organizational Audit, or Reality Check, has two steps. The first is a set of general questions each department must answer. The second is a set of questions specific to each department's functions.

The following questions should lead the entrepreneurial organization toward additional questions that are important to their company. The better the questions, the better the answers.

GENERAL QUESTIONS

- *What is the "chain of command" or departmental structure?*

  Understanding who is accountable to whom and how the players interact is of critical importance when determining future growth strategies.

- *What are the objectives of this department?*

  Each department has specific performance objectives that the organization depends upon to accomplish its goals.

- *What systems are in place to accomplish these objectives?*

  Internal to each department a series of tasks completed in a specific sequence make up a system.

- *What are the tasks in the department?*

  A task or specific function is not completed just so people within a department stay busy. Understanding what people do all day is a question many businesses would like to have answered.

- *Who is accountable for each task?*

  The mere assignment of tasks is not enough. Individuals accountable for the tasks' completion may or may not be the ones responsible for performing the task.

- *Who is responsible for performing each task?*

  Tasks must be done, and who does them is an important realization.

- *Does each task lead to a specific objective?*

  Tasks should lead to specific performance related objectives. Many entrepreneurial organizations tend to keep current systems that are efficient, but lose effectiveness because of the "this is the way we've always done it" mind set.

- *Are there existing teams? What are their specific functions? Do they work?*

- *How do we coordinate with other departments?*

  Specifically how does our work interact with the work of other operating departments. Who are our internal customers and vendors?

- *Do we have established processes and training programs in place so that all employees know the procedures and standards?*

- *Are the employees willing and able to perform their jobs?*

  Determining an employee's "willingness" and/or "ability" to perform tasks allows the organization a way to understand if it needs to use motivation or skills training to improve employee effectiveness.

- *Are systems person-dependent or people-dependent?*

  Entrepreneurial organizations have a propensity to over rely on individual talent in some key areas when it would be better served to have a support system in place.

- *How do employees perceive the entrepreneur and the company?*

  As discussed earlier, entrepreneurs set the tone and the pace of the organization. Entrepreneurs as Visionary Leaders want to know exactly where they stand so they "do the right things."

- *Are employees' needs being met?*

  Often the audit uncovers some very specific areas that with minor adjustments can increase employee productivity based solely upon understanding how their jobs are designed.

- *Do we have the resources needed to perform effectively?*

  Determine the Implementation Strategy Score (ISS) for resource allocation (time, money, people) discussed in Chapter 4.

SPECIFIC QUESTIONS

At this point, each department would be given its own set of questions specific to that department.

OPERATIONS STATUS

Operations is an area that covers manufacturing, production, distribution, warehousing, shipping and receiving, and safety.

Certain vendor relations, purchasing, for example, may also be part of operations. Some organizations may have procurement in other departments.

Some specific points to analyze in the area of Operations are:

- *What is the manufacturing process?*
- *What inventory procedures are used to track raw materials; work in process; and finished goods?*
- *Are our negotiators effective in their relationships with vendors?*
- *Are vendors' quality standards meeting our needs?*
- *Are vendors aware of our raw material needs and timelines?*
- *What is our competitive bid process?*
- *What work flow systems are in place?*
- *Are our technologies up-to-date?*
- *Do we adhere to specific (OSHA) safety standards?*

SALES AND MARKETING STATUS

This area includes advertising and promotions, customer service, public relations, competitive analysis, and new product/service ideas.

Sales and Marketing is usually the entrepreneurs' primary domain, the area where they have the most influence. It is also the function the entrepreneur is most resistant to delegate to others. However, when the various functions are defined, entrepreneurs usually find there are several tasks of which they would gladly yield control.

There is usually an internal paradigm shift during the Sales and Marketing audit. It signals to employees that the business is back on track because the focus is on real competition and external factors—becoming service-driven—not internally on the organization where the attention has been.

Advertising and Promotions

- *How do we advertise our product/service?*
- *Are our advertising and promotion effective? How are results measured?*
- *Do our marketing materials convey a consistent message?*
- *Do potential customers recognize our product names, trademarks, logos and position within our industry?*
- *Who handles Public Relations, and does it meet our expectations?*
- *How effective have our Public Relations efforts been?*

Customer Service

- *Who are our customers? What are their demographics?*
- *Are our customers satisfied? How do we measure their satisfaction?*
- *How do we service them?*
- *How do we attract new customers?*
- *How do we maintain existing customers?*
- *What support services, satisfaction and product warranties do we offer?*
- *Is it easy to buy from us?*
- *What are our terms, how do they compare?*
- *How do we determine sales success?*
- *How are our sales territories divided?*

Competitive Analysis

In order to remain competitive, Visionary Leaders must know what is going on in their industry—who is on the cutting edge and why. Most successful businesses study their competitors on a constant basis.

Entrepreneurial organizations tend to monitor the competition much more closely after they discover the benefits and importance of doing so.

The Reality Check process can focus on the entrepreneurial organization's position in the industry. The results will reveal any shortcomings and highlight any strengths.

Industry Intelligence

- *How do we gather intelligence on industry trends?*
- *What is the current status of our industry? (Growth or decline?)*
- *What projections are being made in the industry?*
- *What are the industry's biggest challenges?*
- *What factors (legislation, environment, consumers) have the most influence on the industry?*
- *Where are we ranked in our industry?*
- *What is our reputation in the industry?*
- *What is our growth compared to industry norms?*

Competitor Intelligence

- *Who are our competitors?*
- *Who is our biggest direct competitor?*
- *Who has what market share?*
- *What are their strengths?*
- *What are their marketing strategies?*
- *Who is using common technologies that are of interest to us?*
- *How do our present strategies, pricing structure, and marketing compare to our competitors?*
- *What tools do we use to assess the competition?*
- *Do we have a procedure for testing competing products?*
- *How are we handling direct challenges to our product or services?*

- *What can we learn from our competitors?*

Customer and Vendor Perceptions

- *How do our customers compare our products to our competitors?*
- *What do our customers think about rival products or services?*
- *Who do they perceive to be our competitors?*
- *What do our suppliers think about rival products or services?*

FINANCE AND ACCOUNTING STATUS

The Reality Check also focuses on the company's financial status and identifies its availability as an effective operating tool. It includes, but is not limited to: accounting, budgeting, cash management, expenditure authorization, and credit policies.

Accounting

This area includes the most commonly associated areas of financial controls such as income statements and balance sheets.

Income statements and balance sheets need to be a timely and accurate reflection of the business. If it is taking three months to get out statements, it is not only difficult to make solid operating decisions, the information may very well be out of date.

- *When are monthly income statements and balance sheets generated?*
- *Who receives them? Reviews them?*
- *Are actual expenditures compared to budgets?*
- *What are considered acceptable actual to budget variances?*
- *When variances occur, what is the procedure for dealing with them?*
- *What is expensed? Capitalized?*

Budgeting

When entrepreneurial organizations have effective budgeting, they have a greater ability to handle cash flow; without it, entrepreneurs are consumed with a money-consciousness. Comparing actual expenditures to budgeting allocations is a critical procedure for determining financial status.

- *Do budgets exist?*
- *How are budgets determined?*
- *Do departmental budgets exist?*
- *Who prepares departmental budgets?*

Authorization for Expenditures

In some companies, only the entrepreneur has this authority—a clear indication that they are in the Benevolent Dictator phase of development.

In other companies, a simple purchase order system has been established and only certain managers have the authority to sign for expenditures—an indication of the Disassociated Director phase.

- *Who authorizes operating expenditures?*
- *Who authorizes capital expenditures?*
- *What is the process for unbudgeted expenditures?*
- *Who is authorized to activate the credit line?*

Cash Flow and Credit

Cash flow is the lifeblood of every company. The average number of days in receivable can seriously impact an organization. For this reason, it is crucial for credit policies and payment terms to acknowledge and reflect the needs of both the customer and the organization.

- *What are the cash management policies?*
- *What is our current cash management system?*

- *What are our payment terms?*
- *What is the average number of days in receivable?*
- *What is acceptable?*
- *What contingency plans are in place? (Credit line, etc.)*
- *What are the current policies for granting credit?*
- *What procedures do we use to check credit?*
- *What are the internal systems for collection?*
- *What are our policies regarding delinquent accounts?*

ADMINISTRATION AND HUMAN RESOURCES STATUS

Administration and Human Resources includes personnel, benefits and compensation, recruiting, hiring, training and education, internal communications, policies, procedures, systems, performance reviews, and employee handbooks.

By looking at Administration, the entrepreneur can determine if employees are able to meet their inner needs as described by Maslow. The organization can then make adjustments to help employees move towards self-actualization.

When employees have structure and organization in their lives, when they know there is a career track, and are provided with attractive benefits and fair compensation, they tend to be more productive workers.

In low-trust organizations employees tend to see compensation, benefits, bonuses, promotions, etc. as owed to them and use them to fulfill safety and security level needs. In high-trust organizations these same items fulfill all the lower level needs and put the individuals at the esteem level.

Personnel

In many entrepreneurial organizations, employees wear several different hats. Of three salespeople at Company Z, one handles customer service, the second concentrates on client contact, and the third prospects for leads. They are key employees with the same title but different duties, therefore creating confusion as to what a salesperson's duties are at Company Z.

By determining the specific role each plays in the department's structure and by defining each contribution with a job description, not only is there less confusion, each is able perform their duties more effectively.

An assessment should be made of each employee's qualifications, their current position and where they fit in the company. Based on the findings, it can be determined if the appropriate talent is in place to move the organization forward.

- *Is there a job description for each position within the organization?*
- *What is the employee orientation process?*
- *How do we recruit and determine qualifications for employment?*
- *What training programs do we provide?*
- *Do we fully understand the role of Human Resources and the federal, state and local laws that effect us?*
- *How do we handle internal communications?*

Compensation and Benefits

Compensation and benefits can be significant motivators. Each employee's satisfaction with this aspect of their job influences their performance and interaction with co-workers and customers, often making the difference between the success or demise of the company.

One way to communicate information to the staff is to create and distribute employee handbooks. Not only do they disburse information, they provide documentation of organizational intent and outline the vehicles for achieving the corporate Mission. Often, the best handbooks are those which have been written by the employees. Participation in creating the policy handbook fulfills the employees' esteem needs as well as their cognitive need to know what is going on in the organization.

Employee handbooks should cover such issues as:

- *Holidays (paid and non-paid)*
- *Vacations*
- *Sick leave and personal time off*
- *Child care*
- *Vesting and profit sharing*
- *Employee grievances and legal problems*
- *Dress code*
- *Reimbursement for expenses*

Some entrepreneurs view employee benefits purely as liabilities because they see them as financial burdens. Yet, benefits are an important part of ongoing success. They can give the entrepreneur the ability to recruit the most qualified people and maintain talented employees.

The emotion-driven entrepreneur tends to reward employees on the basis of personal preferences rather than on consistent and established criteria. If the audit is conducted correctly, while disassociated from emotion, the entrepreneur will be able to rectify tendencies to be less than impartial.

Further questions regarding Benefits and Compensation:

- *What employee benefits are currently in place?*
- *How do we keep track of these benefits?*
- *Are employees satisfied with these benefits?*
- *How are employees compensated? Salary, hourly, commissions?*
- *Is their pay commensurate with their position?*
- *How does the company evaluate employees?*
- *How often are performance reviews conducted?*
- *How are awards, raises and bonuses determined?*
- *How does the entrepreneur view employee benefits?*

Organizational Policies

Many entrepreneurial organizations often wake up to discover that they have fallen into the "Gee, it seemed like a good idea at the time" syndrome. Until entrepreneurs understand *why* they established a particular policy it will not serve them effectively.

Conclusions on whether policies are beneficial and should continue cannot be made until the policies are determined. If employees are unaware of company policies, the organization has a training and communication gap.

Some questions to consider are:

- *What are our current policies?*
- *How does each policy serve the organization?*
- *Have they served the organization well?*
- *Are they oriented toward long-term growth?*
- *Do the policies reflect current needs and trends?*
- *Do we have policy handbooks?*
- *Do the policies reflect the organization's values and style?*
- *Do employees understand the policies?*
- *Do they use them?*

Communication

Visionary Leaders want their employees in the quarry to understand they are building a "Taj Mahal." They want the next in line, those who take delivery of the raw materials and shape them into finished goods, to know that they too can take pride in creating a "Taj Mahal." It isn't only the architect or the builder who is constructing that marvel, ultimate completion hinges on the construction teams and their leaders.

If construction teams are told, through an effective communication system, that they are accountable and responsible for completion of a project that has significance, they feel more empowered and will take pride in their positions and accomplishments. That feeling of pride can echo throughout the organization, enhanced when communication is effective.

Successful entrepreneurial organizations understand the importance of effective communication. Many form teams to achieve the goals and objectives of the company. These teams and departments become communication chains which exchange information in a variety of both formal and informal mediums.

- *What are our current communication strategies?*
- *Do we rely predominately on written or verbal communication?*
- *Is there a central file for internal, written communication?*
- *How often are formal meetings held? Company wide basis? Departmental basis?*
- *Describe the current flow of information*
- *How much information (financial, performance, successes, failures) do we share with the employees?*

Under the Microscope

As entrepreneurs complete the audit, many will realize they have put the company they created under a microscope.

The concluding part of the Reality Check calls for entrepreneurs to put themselves under the microscope as well. It is now time to evaluate:

- *Themselves as Visionary Leaders*
- *Their attitudes, opinions, goals and beliefs about the company*
- *The specific tasks they perform*
- *What they have accomplished*

Most entrepreneurs will find, through the Reality Check, that their organizations are on track in several key areas. When the audit has been completed, the results of the Reality Check can be used as a tool for Strategic Planning which is discussed in Chapter 7.

Chapter 6

Articulating Company Values, Creating Organizational Vision, and Defining Corporate Mission

Ideals are like stars; you will not succeed in reaching them with your hands. But like the seafaring man on the desert of waters, you choose them as your guides, and following them you will reach your destiny.

—Carl Schurz

Even though the path to excellence discussed in this book may seem somewhat unconventional, it is a proven methodology that has produced consistent results in many entrepreneurial enterprises. Humanizing the work environment is one of the components necessary for truly creating excellence in any organization.

Much of today's business literature focuses on values-centered management and principle-centered leadership to accomplish that humanization. By articulating the company's Values, creating an organizational Vision, and defining the corporate Mission, entrepreneurs can transform their existing companies into ones that people desire to work for and with.

Values, or beliefs, drive behavior. They reflect the guiding force behind the actions we take, choices and decisions we make, and behaviors we exhibit. Webster defines Values as "something—

a principle or quality—intrinsically valuable or desirable." When an organization can identify and articulate its Values, define and share them, it has a common reference point from which to view the future.

The organizational Vision is the dream the entrepreneur and the organization are committed to realizing collectively. The Vision inspires both entrepreneurs and employees to join in the pursuit of something meaningful, engaging, and grander than they could accomplish individually.

A compelling Vision provides entrepreneurs with motivation to lead their enterprises into the future. It encompasses the spirit and purpose of the organization and incorporate its humanitarian, idealistic and altruistic goals.

On the other hand, the corporate Mission serves as the benchmark or standard the company is aiming for—the "pragmatic reality" of the Vision. Developed by the entrepreneur in collaboration with their organization, it identifies organizational goals and outlines how they are to be achieved.

When the organization defines and understands its Mission— what business it is in, which products are manufactured, what kind of services are available, and ultimately how business is to be conducted—it is a simple exercise to develop a Strategic Plan and easily assess on a continuing basis whether the organization is truly focused and on track.

Organizations inherently have the potential to withstand the test of time if they share a common purpose that allows them to make the best possible decisions. If everyone is clear about the Values, Vision and Mission, organizational members know where they can make a meaningful contribution. Sharing Values, Vision and Mission creates a sense of community and contributes to a functional and satisfying corporate culture.

Importance of Values, Vision and Mission

Values-based management has gained importance to the business world because the values-driven organization is typically a purpose-driven one. Embodying the beliefs of management and organizational members, values-based management bonds everyone through the application of its principles.

Sharing a common foundation allows entrepreneurial ideals to work synergistically with those of employees, resulting in an organization where everyone understands why they work together and what they are working to accomplish. Values, Vision and Mission enable entrepreneurs to create and manage a truly excellent and successful business.

Operating from this common ground makes it easy to assess if all actions taken within the organization are congruent and within the company's stated principles. It also facilitates movement of individuals and the organization toward accomplishment of goals and objectives.

Hopefully, as companies grow, they continually evolve and change to be more responsive to their marketplace and organizational needs. The Vision and Mission of a company can and should be updated and adjusted periodically to accommodate this natural growth and maturity. Although the organization and circumstances may shift, core Values generally remain constant because the basic tenets by which people live their lives rarely differ.

Values, Vision and Mission as Related to Maslow's Hierarchy of Needs

If Values, Vision and Mission are incorporated into an organization's business practices, they help satisfy most levels of inner needs people must have fulfilled in order to reach full potential and become exceptional performers.

If superior working conditions exist, employees are more apt to strive at becoming self-actualized. Values, Vision and Mission contribute to the nurturing of this environment. In other words, if employees find the workplace to be a source of inspiration where they feel respected and can contribute, they usually produce extraordinary results.

Shared Values satisfy employee needs for belonging because everyone in the organization embraces the same principles, creating a "family" association based on common interests and goals. The Vision accommodates aesthetic needs for order and symmetry by bringing a sense of harmony and beauty to the work environment. The Mission meets cognitive needs of employees to understand and know the ultimate purpose of their activities.

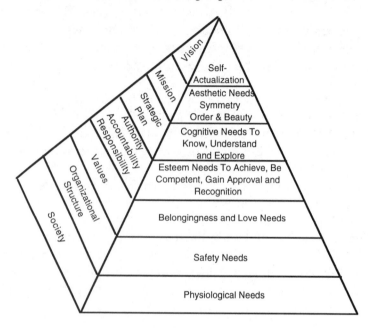

Comparing Maslow's Hierarchy of Needs and the recommendations discussed in this book. Each recommendation fits a specific need for each individual within the entrepreneurial organization.

Articulating Company Values

The personal Values we hold chart our course in life; they provide the navigational tools we need for reaching our destination. When organizational members share similar personal Values, those Values act as a pathway to help people of like minds accomplish great deeds together.

Shared Values create understanding and facilitate teamwork. If team members discover common Values, they can more effectively focus on the planned direction of the organization. Realizing they are working to accomplish goals and objectives from a common ground generates good feelings and creates a sense of community.

Articulating, discussing and prioritizing the Values of the company can create the guidelines for establishing the strategic focus, goals and objectives. If entrepreneurs and employees stay within an agreed-upon set of Values, decision making is greatly simplified.

These guidelines exist and can be referred to in determining what may be the best choice in a given situation. Conflicts are reduced significantly when people work toward common goals and clearly understand and trust the motives and intentions of their colleagues.

Identifying Company Values

Values represent the very foundation of a business; therefore, they must be selected to reflect the organization's optimum opportunity. Asking each employee to identify their personal Values is useful in determining company Values. If employees are to contribute and prosper within the organization, entrepreneurs must ensure everyone is operating from the same Values base.

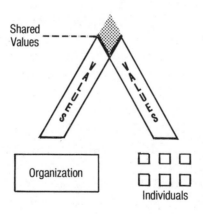

As the organization discovers its shared values it will discover how people can more effectively work together and re-discover why they are working together.

As many people tend to include honesty, integrity and freedom as personal Values, they may choose to work in a particular environment that embraces those same Values organizationally.

Process of Articulating Company Values

Entrepreneurs and employees can reach consensus on their shared Values by working through the following process:

Step 1

Entrepreneurs begin by identifying their own personal Values—listing the qualities and principles most meaningful and important to them and then jotting down a few reasons why these particular qualities and principles are valued.

Step 2

The entrepreneur then inventories what they believe are the Values held by those within the organization. Even though this inventory will probably be very similar to the entrepreneur's personal one, it provides a good reality check later for the entrepreneur to assess how well their individual perceptions match with the organization's.

Step 3

Next, the entrepreneur, senior managers and employees generate a list together. Many Values may appear repeatedly; others may surface that are definitely unique. By combining and refining ideas, the final version can appropriately reflect the shared Values while still respecting the diversity of all participating.

Step 4

Finally, the organization prioritizes the shared Values and reaches consensus on the definition of what each means in an organizational context. Through rank ordering, the shared Values becomes a hierarchical standard that the organization can then hold to and live by.

Benefits of Articulating Company Values

Visionary Leaders nurture an environment for others to identify and articulate a shared set of Values; they do not impose their own beliefs on others. Involving others creates cohesiveness within the organization and secures a willingly accepted standard for interaction.

As the organization engages in this process, participants develop a greater appreciation for colleagues and the value each adds to the organization. This process also expands perspectives and incorporates diverse points of view, enhancing everyone's ability to see the world through another window. In the process, key words tend to turn up on a consistent basis such as "commitment," "creation," "truth," "balance," "honesty," "integrity," and "make a difference."

During this exercise, entrepreneurs and employees often discover they are confusing the importance placed on something with its worth. An additional benefit of articulating company Values is realizing *Values* and *priorities* can be quite different. Even though this may create conflict and cause confusion, it contributes to overall understanding and learning.

Once these core Values have been identified, it is important they be clearly articulated. Verbal explanations are not sufficient. The Values must be documented so everyone understands the definition and priority of each.

As different meanings exist for words depending on the person and the context, defining the terms used to express a specific Value creates shared meaning. When everyone appreciates they are in this together, most of the energy and effort spent on infighting can be channeled and redirected into creating a more effective organization, superior products, and a conducive work environment.

An Example of Articulated Company Values

It is often useful for the novice exploring this process to see what other organizations have generated as company Values. For instance, the stated Values of the author's organization are as follows:

Truth

We stand for and can be measured by our total and uncompromising commitment to truth, honesty and integrity.

Value

Our clients receive value greater than their investment in our services. We determine that value by the three-dimensional wins we create.

Difference

We have the ability to contribute to each individual, group or company we have contact with. We make significant efforts to protect the environment. We are committed to making a difference in the quality of our lives and that of others.

Freedom

We choose our path and have the power to always live at cause. We are a part of the universe; it is a part of us.

Fun

We balance our lives with joy in our hearts. We are optimistic and see the good in everything the world has to offer.

*****

The benefit of sharing core Values, or philosophies, is it becomes the culture for the organization. If employees are treated well, then they will likely treat clients and suppliers in the same way.

While cash flow and profits are often high priorities, many entrepreneurial organizations find when they articulate company Values, financial gain is not anywhere close to the top of the list. In fact, entrepreneurs are often astounded to find the creation of wealth is not among the top ten, even though financial concerns often consume much of their time and energy.

Employees are attracted to organizations that value people; in turn, people are the most important asset an organization can possess. A benefit of identifying and articulating a company's Values is in the increased ability to recruit key employees.

On the other hand, a phenomenon that occurs while discovering company Values is called natural self-selection. As employees engage in the Values-articulating exercise, which eventually leads to defining the corporate Mission, they may decide they no longer wish to be a part of the organization and may opt to leave the company.

Although respecting this choice is difficult, it is one that must be accepted. Entrepreneurial enterprises do not have the luxury of dragging organizational members along who are not committed to the same Vision and do not share the common Values. By wishing them well and allowing them to leave with dignity, they can find opportunities that will, in fact, give their lives more purpose and meaning.

Creating Organizational Vision

Fixing your objective is like identifying the North Star, you sight your compass on it and then use it as a means of getting back on track when you tend to stray.

–Marshall E. Dimock

Organizational Vision represents the compelling reason for existence and draws the company into the future. The Vision reflects the dreams, aspirations and hopes of the organization and the people within it. It is almost a spiritual concept in that it lights the pathway of shared Values, creates unity, and bonds the entrepreneur and employees together to achieve a mutual purpose.

Developing a compelling organizational Vision is a process that involves focus on the part of both the entrepreneur and the organization. Fulfilling the Vision becomes the driving force of the organization. Understanding the Vision and the commitment to it helps each individual within the organization make decisions that have real impact upon its attainment.

The Vision enhances operating and allocation-of-resource decisions because people are clear on what is important. Strategic and tactical decisions can be measured against the "real" future of the organization—its Vision.

Clarity of purpose and focused action must be the ultimate priorities; otherwise resources become scattered, dissipating time and energy. If this happens, the Vision will have little likelihood of ever becoming a reality. For these reasons, no organization can pursue more than one Vision at a time.

The Visioning process can be completed in a reasonable time frame provided the entrepreneur and the organization are committed to creating a shared dream together.

A series of questions helpful to the Visioning process are listed below. These questions are meant only as a guide. There are many "right" ways to create organizational Vision. The most vital component is a shared belief in the Vision once it has been articulated.

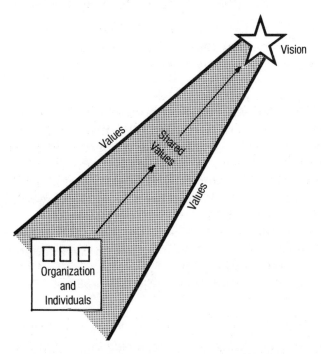

The shared values form the path towards the future, with the organizational vision lighting the way.

As answers are compiled, key phrases will repeat and form patterns. These patterns of words are common denominators in the creation of the final Vision statement. These words and phrases often contain many of the company Values earlier identified. This is a key indicator the entrepreneur and the organization are tracking one another.

The words that make up the Vision statement need to be powerful and inspiring. The statement itself should provide a real stretch for the organization. Gathering individual input and ideas in a written Vision statement should engage and excite everyone. This "driving force" becomes the "beckoning light" everyone is committed to realizing.

Where there is no vision, the people perish.
                                        –Bible, Proverbs 29:18

It is important to consider the three questions Peter Drucker suggests all companies ask themselves:

- *What business are we in?*
- *What business will we be in?*
- *What business should we be in?*

A clear understanding of the answers to Drucker's questions enhance an organization's ability to meet its future challenges. Visioning looks at all three with a specific emphasis on "What business should we be in?" Many companies "forget" what business they are in and why they exist. Profit is not and cannot be the only motive. People need meaningful work and expect more from companies today than ever before.

Organizations that successfully answer these questions and the ones that follow are uniquely positioned to lead their industries in the future.

Questions the entrepreneur and the organization must address include:

- *What do customers know about us and our organization?*
- *All things being equal, what would we want to be known for?*
- *What do we really value?*
- *How will we conduct ourselves and our business in the future?*
- *What do we hope to achieve?*
- *What will be our priorities?*
- *What excites us and keeps us focused?*
- *Will this "statement" stretch and motivate us to act?*

Samples of Organizational Vision

Systemic Formulas, Inc.

Stuart Wheelwright, founder and president, provided these comments regarding the Visioning process:

The most inspiring, frustrating, creative, confusing and exciting process we have done as a company. We truly believe in our Vision.

We have put out to the universe what we are working toward, and we are accomplishing our goals quicker and more easily than ever.

Our Vision statement reflects our intentions as an organization. It's a nice feeling to know we are all committed to the same purpose.

Systemic Formulas' Vision statement reads as follows:

Systemic Formulas is dedicated to being a recognized world leader in Nutritional Wellness based on high ethics and sound principles of Integrity, Quality, Safety and Honesty ultimately leading to the Systemic Wellness Lifestyle.

"My organization now uses [our] shared Values along with the Vision statement as a constant reminder of what behaviors we truly are willing to accept from each other, our customers and our vendors. Sales and customer satisfaction have soared. Our distributors are excited about working with a company that is making a qualitative difference in the way people choose to live their lives."

Citizens Against Crime, Inc.

The largest franchising seminar company in the United States generated the following Vision statement for themselves and their franchisees:

Through passionate commitment to integrity and wholeness, we will be a leader in creating a path empowering and supporting people to take responsible action that positively impacts the quality of life.

The above statement also incorporates their articulated company Values of integrity, passion, commitment, responsibility, empowerment, and quality of life. As this organization is a franchisor, the company's Vision of impacting quality of life carries over to the franchisees and, in turn, to customers. This Vision statement is both humanitarian yet practical, stating strategies they plan to implement.

Organizations that have Vision statements and proudly share them make a declaration to be held accountable and demonstrate they are willing to "walk their talk."

Defining Corporate Mission

While the Vision encompasses the spirit of the organization and its Visionary Leader, the Mission is a document that defines and communicates the more immediate goals and objectives of the company. One of the prime benefits of defining corporate Mission is that of providing a yardstick, or reality check, against which results can be measured.

To develop a Mission statement for an entrepreneurial organization, the same process is used that created the organizational Vision. However, this time goals replace purpose. The process is somewhat easier than creating the Vision because whereas the Vision required people to "stretch," defining the Mission is a more pragmatic, less emotional exercise.

The Quarry Workers' Mission

An example of the benefits of understanding a Mission is the tale of three quarry workers from different organizations who were breaking rocks. Each was asked what they were doing.

The first, who was working slowly and angrily, answered: "breaking rocks." The second, not much happier, replied: "making building stones." The third worker, happily smashing rocks with enthusiasm and accomplishing twice the amount of work of the other two, explained: "I'm helping to build a cathedral."

The third quarry worker was working with a purpose. He took pride in his work, feeding his esteem and cognitive needs to know, understand and explore. His belief in the value of his contribution helped to empower him toward self-actualization.

While the quarry worker may have been light years removed from senior management, his actions were focused because he was as knowledgeable about the Vision and Mission as those at the top. A pragmatic understanding and the reality of taking focused action to attain the corporate Mission empowers each and every individual within the organization.

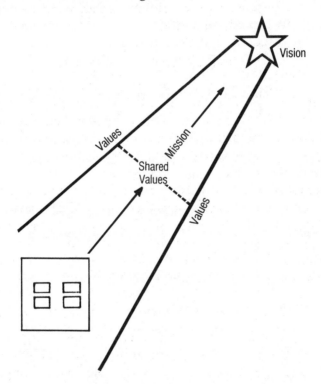

The Mission keeps the organization focused and on the correct path.

Examples of Corporate Mission Statements

The Mission statement for Entrepreneurial Development Group is:

Transforming entrepreneurial visions and intentions into organizational realities and results.

The Mission of the franchisor discussed earlier reads as follows:

This company is dedicated to positive results built upon clear direction, timely communication and follow-through on commitments.

When the organization conceived the above statement, the entire company lacked follow-through on its commitments. There was no clear direction and agreements were often "forgotten or modified."

After articulating the company Values, creating an organizational Vision, and defining corporate Mission, they stated their major goals and objectives as follows:

- *Attaining positive results*
- *Focusing with clear direction and a specific plan of action that includes performance expectations*
- *Communicating in a timely fashion to disseminate information to employees, suppliers and customers*
- *Becoming a leader in the field while empowering and supporting franchisees*

The organization has subsequently become the largest franchisor of its market segment in the United States and is a model for other organizations to emulate.

In addition to the corporate Mission, departments should develop their own Mission statement. These departmental statements are generated through the same process as the corporate Mission statement was; however, they are more specific to the individuals comprising that department. Departmental Mission statements ultimately must lead to the attainment of the corporate Mission. Any organization using a Vision and Mission process should encourage departments to define their Missions.

The productivity of a work group seems to depend on how the group members see their own goals in relation to the goals of the organization.

–Paul Hersey

What's Next?

Once the guidelines of Values have been articulated for organizational behavior and the Vision and Mission statements are in place, the entrepreneur and the organization are ready to focus on the real work of "how to get where they are going."

Expecting everyone within the organization to "walk the talk" allows the organization to become healthier and engenders a more productive work environment. Those associated with the organization have a clear understanding as to what the company stands for and believes in which is really the essence of what constitutes the ultimate success of an enterprise.

Life is either a daring adventure or nothing.
                                                    –Helen Keller

Chapter 7

Developing The Strategic Plan:
Blueprint for the Future

The future belongs to those who believe in the beauty of their dreams.

—Eleanor Roosevelt

In successful organizations, Strategic Planning is an on-going business practice. A skillfully developed action or game plan can result in victory over the competition and a win/win/win scenario for everyone; a lack of strategy can lose the battle on all fronts.

The Strategic Plan offers entrepreneurs a pro-active tool for establishing and accomplishing corporate goals and objectives. It articulates the steps along the pathway to achieve the corporate Mission by specifying how to reach the goals and effectively manage the organization.

When entrepreneurial enterprises have a well-devised and comprehensive Strategic Plan, they are equipped to move confidently toward the future. In this way, the organization can determine the specific tactics (action steps) needed, agree upon the suitable levels of authority, accountability and responsibility and then assign the functional tasks required to accomplish the goals and objectives.

*The **preparation** of an annual plan is in itself the end, not the resulting bound volume....To prepare and justify [a plan], people go through a lot of soul-searching analysis and juggling, and it is this mental exercise that is valuable.*

—Andrew S. Grove

The process of developing the Strategic Plan is just as important as the Plan it generates. To be comprehensive, the Plan must represent a variety of perspectives including those of employees. In addition to fulfilling esteem and cognitive needs on Maslow's pyramid, employee involvement and contribution to the planning process benefits the organization because members share "ownership" for the ultimate design.

A Strategic Plan enables the organization to make decisions consistent with intended goals and within articulated Values. When the Strategic Plan has been developed and execution begins, it is then possible to purposefully manage the organization and truly strengthen and empower employees.

During the Reality Check, the Decision Making Process Model was used to assess the current status of the organization. By employing the same Process Model during the development of the Strategic Plan, the organization can shift its focus appropriately from the present to the future.

Benefits of Strategic Planning

The major benefit of the Strategic Planning process is in enabling the entrepreneurial organization to become a service- or purpose-driven enterprise. The Strategic Plan allows everyone to understand the company's reason for being in business so when priorities are determined and listed in the Plan, employees appreciate how every function is oriented to a common purpose.

There is nothing so useless as doing efficiently that which should not be done at all.

—Peter Drucker

When a company is focused on serving the best interests of the customer, it is neither sales- nor operations-driven. There are no unnecessary or dramatic pendulum swings because the Strategic Plan defines how sales and operations are to be conducted and coordinated to create a delicate balance.

Strategic Planning also encourages entrepreneurial organizations to think long-term to ensure that the company can withstand the test of time. When the Plan contains the structure, policies, procedures and systems to support its implementation and a means for modifying the Plan when necessary to remain competitive, the odds are much greater the company will thrive and grow.

In addition to producing specific tactical and action plans, Strategic Planning trains entrepreneurs and employees in the intricacies of coordinating a variety of tasks, functions and resources. It guides and enables various departments to create a cohesive strategy for attaining the intended outcomes.

Everything someone does should be traceable back to an annual or quarterly plan.

—Richard E. Griggs

Value of Documenting the Strategic Plan

The Strategic Plan must be documented and communicated in order to create a more effective organization. The Strategic Planning process reinforces commitment to realizing organizational Vision and accomplishing the corporate Mission. The Strategic Plan often becomes the operating "bible" and serves continuously as a point of reference for the organization.

The written form of the Strategic Plan provides tangible, physical evidence that the entrepreneur and the organization are serious about producing the desired results together. If organizational members know what the expectations are and understand the time frames for meeting those expectations, they can easily gauge if their actions and choices contribute to the achievement of goals and objectives.

The Plan assists the entrepreneur in managing the organization by ensuring everyone knows the rules and follows the same game plan. By the same token, the organization is virtually guaranteed the "talk will be walked" or the credibility of the entrepreneur is at risk.

Financial institutions know their investment is more secure if they invest in businesses that have demonstrated they "plan their work and work their plan." For this very reason, they insist on having documented plans submitted before they consider loaning capital to an organization.

Strategic Planning as a Vehicle for Enhancing the "Three Cs"

Visionary Leaders understand their business must fulfill specific customer needs while at the same time satisfying the higher, internal needs of employees. Allowing employees to take part in the process of creating the Strategic Plan is an important management tool, embodying the three components of Visionary Leadership—communication, cooperation and collaboration.

Communication allows individuals to feel competent, gain recognition and demonstrate their abilities. When defining specific job responsibilities, the person best qualified to participate in devising tactics to accomplish the goals is the person who holds that position.

Cooperation brings employees to the cognitive level by including them in the process so they can determine how their skills fit in. Employee needs to explore are satisfied by looking at alternatives, suggesting options, and subsequently selecting the best course of action.

Collaboration helps sustain the employees' cognitive needs by allowing empowerment to truly take hold within the organization. As employees continue to perform at these higher levels, a natural "team effect" occurs when employees feel a real sense of pride and satisfaction in their organizational roles and contributions.

The policies, procedures and systems designed to support the Strategic Plan fulfill employee needs for symmetry, order and beauty provided the Strategic Plan is fully implemented and the tactics are well executed.

The Strategic Plan—An Architectural Blueprint

The development of a Strategic Plan for accomplishing organizational goals and objectives is akin to creating architectural blueprints for an edifice or structure. Creating a Strategic Plan allows participants to imagine what the structure will look like, identify what it will be used for, understand why it is designed in a particular style and appreciate how their specific contributions add value.

The successful organization must have a solid foundation able to withstand the pressure—weight—exerted upon it as the construction unfolds. The greater the magnitude of the building, the more complex and sophisticated the blueprints. Unfortunately, many entrepreneurial organizations fall apart because the cornerstones—the entrepreneurs—are unable to support the weight of the organization, at least until they become Visionary Leaders.

Creating the Strategic Plan is like designing a vast, new corporate headquarters with state-of-the-art architecture and steel and glass towers commanding the skyline. The building must be functionally designed so employees can handle their work easily.

Before ground can be broken, the necessary building permits must be secured. The contractor refers to the blueprints to know exactly how the structure is to be built and how the components fit together. The total project expenses are estimated and financial needs and resources assessed. The number of workers and other specialists to support the project are determined and hired.

The architect and the contractor collaborate. With the blueprint as the guide, they determine the amount of raw materials needed to meet the specifications and calculate how much equipment will be required for completion of the structure.

Like the architectural blueprints and renderings, the Strategic Plan must consider the various components to be executed simultaneously and determine the priorities and steps necessary to accomplish this feat. The Strategic Plan provides blueprint specifications and information for the entrepreneurial organization.

Participation in the Process

You can dream, create, design, and build the most wonderful place in the world, but it requires people to make the dream a reality.

—Walt Disney

Traditionally, Strategic Plans have been the product of senior management or a staff hired for that purpose. Visionary Leaders, who are less bound by tradition, engage every level of the organization in the planning process. Allowing everyone to participate ensures all perspectives are taken into account. Visionary Leaders share decision making which empowers employees and brings individual strengths to the construction of the organization.

Successful Strategic Plans are flexible rather than rigid, permitting changes to be made if necessary to accommodate the fluid marketplace or other influences affecting organizational activities. Ongoing measurements in the Strategic Plan indicate when and where the organization should consider making a shift.

Involving everyone ensures that they will understand how to execute any modifications to the Strategic Plan. Through the Strategic Planning vehicle, the entire organization can share ownership for its development and, therefore, be more fully committed to attaining its goals and objectives and the corporate Mission it encompasses.

Creating Appropriate Structures

The entrepreneurial organization must be careful when developing and implementing the Strategic Plan to add enough structure to support the corporate Mission but not so much the organization becomes bureaucratic and inflexible.

Entrepreneurial organizations need to provide enough structure so employees can excel at their jobs. Once excellence has been achieved in the appropriate skill levels, the organization may experiment with new and improved structures. However, experimentation should be attempted only after evidence of excellence has been clearly demonstrated.

The entrepreneurial organization may decide to reshape or modify its structure if the existing structure doesn't support current goals. When creating a new structure, it is important to remember the company must understand how finances, resources and service to customers will be affected before implementing the changes.

Visionary Leaders often depart from traditional businesses in structuring their organizations. As discussed in Chapter 3, they position themselves, senior management and the Board of Directors at the foundation in order to support the entire structure. Visionary Leaders understand the customer belongs at the apex and they build their organization to reflect that belief.

While this structure is inverted, this does not mean that decision making continues to be pushed onto the entrepreneur or senior managers. Rather this structure is designed so people at appropriate levels have the autonomy to make and execute decisions to support the Strategic Plan.

A structural component of the Strategic Plan is the determination of who will have authority, accountability and responsibility for each job function. Employees who are given authority, accountability and responsibility are more productive because their higher needs are being met. This positive attitude can, and usually does, result in wins for the employee, the company and the customer.

Developing the Strategic Plan

The initial process of creating a Strategic Plan and capturing it on paper may appear complicated. The process involves many components which are interrelated and simultaneously executed.

The process is highly interactive. It involves everyone in the organization in some way, giving employees the opportunity to communicate, cooperate and collaborate. Every person in the entrepreneurial enterprise has a stake in the Strategic Plan. Their collective action, therefore, is vital to its success.

Nothing creates more self-respect among employees than being included in the process of decision making.
—Judith M. Bardwick

To begin the process, Visionary Leaders may establish a design team to facilitate the development of the Strategic Plan. Team members typically consist of senior management, directors, department heads, managers, supervisors, line employees, and those dealing directly with vendors and customers. The diversity of the team enables it to consider the needs and requirements of planning and decision making from all aspects within the company and externally from customer and vendor perspectives.

When the Planning teams are formed and departments communicate directly with each other, the team concept can provide the opportunity to work out ways to quickly remedy situations or create solutions for common problems via sharing information and ideas.

Many of the components of the Strategic Plan have already been created through the process of articulating the corporate Values, Vision and Mission. The Reality Check established the baseline for determining the current status and identifying immediate needs.

Another component of the Plan considers the internal conditions affecting the company's viability. For instance, a Strategic Analysis of the expected capabilities of the organization in terms of resources and departmental objectives and policies should be developed in agreement with the corporate strategies and tactics.

Other components such as policies, procedures, systems and tasks support the structure of the organization, satisfy Maslow's "higher needs" theory and define what must be done (as well as how) to bring the Strategic Plan to fruition.

Quite simply, policies, procedures, processes, systems and tasks define the organization's order of business. Without them, no one is ever sure of the company's priorities nor are they prepared to help the company attain its goals and objectives. Let's take a closer look at how this structure is applied:

- *If the company makes it a Policy to provide total customer satisfaction,*

- *A Procedure should then be established detailing how employees in all departments are to do their jobs in order to provide total customer satisfaction.*

- *A Process would then emerge outlining the work flow, illustrating the functional interdependency between the various departments, and explaining how that interdependency is vital to reaching the company's goal of total customer satisfaction.*

- *The work flow described above is composed of Systems. A System is actually a series of jobs that lead to a combined outcome and the various Systems within the company flow together to create a Process.*

- *The components of a System are the Tasks, or specific job duties performed by each employee.*

Once policies, procedures, processes, systems and tasks have been established, the authority, accountability and responsibility (AAR) for them must be assigned. The tools for constructing policies, procedures, processes, systems and tasks include the "Three Cs" (communication, cooperation and collaboration), the Decision Making Process Model and the assignment of appropriate AAR.

What Can Be Controlled—What Cannot

While the organization may not have power over all external factors and the general business climate, the Strategic Plan can prepare the company for varying conditions and ensure control of its service to customers at all times.

Businesses planned for service are apt to succeed; businesses planned for profit are apt to fail.

—Nicholas M. Butler

Economic fluctuations, instability in the marketplace and new competition are among the external factors the design team can strategically plan to handle. With the help of the Decision Making Process Model, the team can conduct the Strategic Analysis to help the organization make choices about how it will respond to the marketplace given various possible circumstances.

There is great value in creating "what if . . ." scenarios while in the process. Doing so enables the entrepreneurial organization to understand whether it has the capacity to develop new business and diversify and match competitors. Knowing the potential consequences and operating components of various situations allows the organization to assess where the greatest return will be on the resources expended.

The Strategic Analysis may include evaluation of new product ideas with regards to market needs to determine if they are congruent with the Strategic Plan and the corporate Mission. If opportunities and goals complement each other, strategies and tactics can then be devised to facilitate their achievement.

Determining Goals and Objectives

In the Strategic Plan, goals and objectives guide the entrepreneurial organization toward achieving its corporate Mission. They represent benchmarks and milestones the company will attain as the Plan is executed. With specific goals and objectives defined, it will then be possible to create individual job functions to support the accomplishment of those goals and objectives.

Goals may be defined as a series of long-range intentions, such as working toward a certain percentage of growth, higher profits or better quality products and services. Goals consider both the pragmatic realities of the marketplace and the capabilities of the company.

Objectives are simply organizational goals expressed in measurable terms, to be achieved within the Strategic Plan's time frame. Think of corporate objectives as stepping stones along the path that leads toward the organization's ultimate goal.

Bold objectives require conservative engineering.
—James E. Webb

Successful entrepreneurial organizations create both primary and secondary goals and objectives. Each goal should work in synergy with every other goal and must be articulated, communicated and understood. When entrepreneurs and the organization know what the corporate goals are, each department can then specify actions that will be required to reach the overall goals.

Visionary Leaders must ensure goals and objectives are within the company Values, move toward realizing the organizational Vision and accomplish the corporate Mission. Some companies establish goals that are impossible to attain; this sets up the organization to fail. Goals and objectives that are realistic, within reason, clear and important will receive more attention and usually be accomplished more often than those perceived to be unattainable.

It is advisable to conduct a periodic and intense review of the specific goals and objectives to ensure they keep the organization moving in the designated direction. Often goals may actually work at odds with each other like trying to increase sales by 25% while decreasing travel, entertainment and promotional expenses by the same amount.

Designing for Success

The organizational members must be able to visualize success. To achieve this, smaller, interim goals can be identified at various stages of the strategy which ultimately lead to accomplishing the final goal. In this way, employees have the opportunity to celebrate successes all along the way.

People with goals succeed because they know where they are going.

—Earl Nightingale

Some companies focus first on a few priority goals and build everything toward attaining them, making sure each of the support functions lead directly to goal achievement. As they grow more competent and their wins increase, those same companies then tackle a greater span of goals.

Most employees feel more empowered to achieve organizational goals if they are given decision making powers and some autonomy when developing their portions of the Strategic Plan. It is recommended, however, that every objective be specific enough to be measurable so performance and direction can be gauged accurately.

When Will We Arrive?

Time frames are a key element in the Strategic Plan. By determining realistic schedules and accurately predicting the attendant consequences, the result is reaching goals more often.

The success of most things depends upon knowing how long it would take to succeed.
                              —Charles de Secondat Montesquieu

A timely, effective system for measuring organizational progress lets everyone know whether or not they are on track. This system must be established to measure variables at different stages of the development.

When drawing up a Strategic Plan, it is tempting to concentrate on short-term, quick-profit objectives. These objectives can ease a current financial shortfall, yet they rarely solve the problems of continual income generation over the long-term.

A farmer who has 12 eggs, sells them all in one day and eats chicken for dinner is less likely to have a steady year-round income than the farmer who sells half of his eggs and keeps the remaining six to be hatched into more chickens to lay more eggs!

Understanding the Focuses of the Strategic Plan

When determining long-term strategic objectives, there are several major areas to consider:

- *Personnel Development*
- *Employee Productivity*

- *Operating Strategies*
- *Profits*
- *The Business Environment*
- *Competitive Position*
- *New Business Opportunities*

Personnel Development

The specific competitive advantage of all businesses are and will be created and designed by people. It is the responsibility of every entrepreneur and organization to invest in its most important and critical asset—its people.

Employee Productivity

Employee productivity and profits are interdependent. If employees are self-actualized, they are productive; if they are not, productivity and profits suffer. Establishing standards of productivity is a way to measure employee performance and can be an objective in and of itself. Employees who are given the opportunity to be productive and meet goals and objectives are better prepared to be peak performers.

Operating Strategies

Operating Strategies determine how the action plan will be implemented. Functional strategies transfer thought and plan into action. Strategies provide guidance and direction. Every function leading to the accomplishment of the corporate Mission is listed during the planning process. Also identified and assigned during the process are the authority, accountability and responsibility for each action coupled with a description of the objectives.

Operating Strategies spell out to organizational members the systems, policies, procedures and tasks that will be needed to put the Plan into action. For instance, in the marketing area, key efforts are built around the "Four Ps:"

1. *Product*
2. *Promotion*
3. *Pricing*
4. *Placement*

Product covers the development, improvement or modification of products and services. Promotion includes every factor affecting the marketing of products and services. Pricing relates to the financial controls. Placement is defined as anything related to product shipping and distribution.

Thus, during the process of creating the Strategic Plan, the team considers everything influencing or affecting the "Four Ps."

Profits

The fuel keeping the corporate engine running is clearly obtained through profits. When profit objectives are strategically planned, they enhance the entrepreneurial organization's ability to conduct and remain in business. Profits alone are not what being in business is all about; yet, without them, staying in business is improbable.

The Business Environment

Setting objectives concerning the environment takes into consideration the company's relationship with the community, government and society in general. Long-term objectives need to remain flexible so they can be modified or changed to reflect the influence of internal and external events.

Competitive Position

The entrepreneurial organization should know from the Reality Check what their competitive position is in the industry. Having this information can be helpful in creating long-term objectives to maintain or improve upon that position.

New Business Opportunities

The capacity of an organization to survive and financially prosper is dependent on its abilities to innovate and sell first to its existing market niche to ensure customer loyalty. This capacity must continually expand while looking for new business opportunities for creating new customers.

Developing Tactics and Planning for Future Growth

The basic reasons for businesses to exist are to attract and retain customers. Growing a business is the outcome of successful performance. The only way to build a business is by increasing the number of new customers while developing strategically-planned tactics to keep those existing customers satisfied and purchasing products or services again and again.

Entrepreneurial companies should systematically discover the set of conditions best for growing the organization as each enterprise and product or service is unique. Rarely can a game plan be applicable to more than one enterprise, although the same basic equipment—tools, techniques and components—may be used to create the Strategic Plan.

Who Does What by When?

When determining tactics, the question of authority, accountability and responsibility arises. The entrepreneur and the organization must decide who will have the authority, accountability and responsibility for each function and task, to whom they report and why.

It is important to also determine what the consequences will be for performance or non-performance. This determination is critical in attaining communication, cooperation and ultimately collaboration. Consequences for performance or non-performance require discussion and agreement by each member of the team with the caveat that a consequence does not mean it is negative in nature.

A consequence of a 100% increase in sales may result in a need for more working capital to purchase raw materials, refining distribution procedures, increasing work loads of existing personnel or adding employees.

A significant difference between a Strategic Plan and a Business Plan is the amount of information making its way to the operating staffs. As mentioned earlier, many bankers ask for Business Plans to help them determine the credit worthiness of a company. Although the major components may be identical, the specifications of tactics, time frames and "realities" will be much more detailed in a Strategic Plan.

The financial planning function of the Strategic Plan includes pro forma financial projections of expected sales and expenses. These financial projections must be based in reality. A good rule of thumb is to "expect the best and plan for the worst."

Venture capitalists have some very standard rules for handling new business requests for money when they look at the pro forma financial projections. They cut the sales number in half and double the expenses. Additionally, it is not uncommon for them to increase the expected time frames for project completion; most venture capitalists find entrepreneurs to be optimistic to a fault.

We discussed earlier the entrepreneur's propensity to over-promise and under-deliver. Be very careful this does not occur during the Strategic Planning process. Financial controls must be a part of every successful business and accounted for in any Strategic Plan if the Plan is to be effective.

Sales forecasts should be based on some logical rationale and must be realistic. Budgets are tools to help operating mangers make critical decisions. Without good financial information, businesses are doomed to fail. Operating budgets must include contingency plans for times of abundance as well as times of austerity.

The ability of an organization to plan its work and work its plan dictates the success of the enterprise. Ability is a skill. With proper training, skills can be increased.

A Case Study Example

After one company in the Midwest completed the Strategic Planning process, they decided to focus their efforts and resources on the following:

1. *Uncovering unrealized markets*
2. *Expanding the size of their existing market*
3. *Increasing the purchasing power of an existing customer*
4. *Developing product innovations*
5. *Exploring process innovations*
6. *Defining competitive advantages*

These six focuses resulted in a 300% increase in new sales over a 24-month period of time and an even greater increase in repeat orders from existing customers.

In order to support the increase in sales, operating expenditures went up slightly. However, due to new vendor relationships and technological improvements, the company also saw a 35% decrease in the cost of goods sold.

Implementing The Plan

If the Strategic Plan of an organization is similar to the architectural blueprints for a major construction project, understanding the importance of each component is crucial.

Setting realistic time frames for taking ideas from creation to implementation is a difficult concept for most entrepreneurs. At this point in the development of the company, patience is absolutely critical.

Planning involves looking at the organization from as many angles as possible and means committing the resources available to accomplishing the Plan. Resources include good people, money and time—the three assets every organization needs most.

Managing in accordance with a strategic plan is a learned art. The longer you use the tool, the better you are able to manage with it.

—R. Henry Miglione

Chapter 8

Conclusion:
Realizing the Dream

*Manage your organization for what you want it to become. . .
not for what it is and never for what it was.*
                                        —Roy F. Cammarano

Throughout this book you have seen how entrepreneurial behavior ultimately determines the success or failure of an organization. Perhaps no other influence is as vital, nor has the impact, as does the behavior of the entrepreneur.

Behavior, as used here, is an all-encompassing entity which includes attitude, style of communication, management and leadership, decision making, and the treatment of employees, customers and vendors.

True, the behavior each entrepreneur exhibits and the path each entrepreneur takes will be determined, in part, by the organization's Values, Vision and Mission. But the desire and the willingness to behave in a positive manner must come from the entrepreneur's heart. For without internal commitment followed by appropriate, positive behavior, the best-laid plans will fall by the wayside.

The fact that you have selected this book and made the effort to read it through to the end signifies that you have the desire, interest and commitment to do what's best for your organization. And while it is true that entrepreneurs can change the world, sometimes the first step has to be a willingness to change themselves.

Now that you have made the commitment to changing your behavior, perhaps the most important tools at your disposal are the "Three Cs": communication, cooperation and collaboration. To that, we might add the fourth "C": consistency—the cornerstone of Trust.

If the entrepreneur and the entire organizational team communicate and trust each other, if the entrepreneur behaves in a consistent manner and the employees know where they fit in, if the needs of the employees are met, if everyone cooperates as part of a committed and dedicated team, then the entrepreneur and the organization can truly collaborate, thereby attaining the highest level of success.

Of course, it is not easy to reach that level of success and many entrepreneurial organizations struggle through some growing pains along the way. However, now that you have the tools and the willingness to apply them, you, and more importantly your organization, will be able to avoid much of the significant pain caused by misdirected entrepreneurial behaviors. No matter what entrepreneurial phase you are in, you can bypass the pain and move right into the role of Visionary Leader.

Perhaps one of the most noticeable stumbling blocks is failure to understand the total role of the employees in the organization and that in order for them to be productive, they must also feel fulfilled. Understanding the needs of the employees and seeing how meeting or not meeting those needs affect the employees' work habits, is vital to the organization's success.

Early in the development of the company, entrepreneurial commitment, passion and charisma were sufficient to satisfy most employee needs and allowed organizational members to reach their full potential. As you will recall from your reading, entrepreneurs, as natural leaders, tend to over-lead and under-manage. In other words, enthusiasm filled in a lot of holes.

According to Maslow's paradigm for the hierarchy of needs, the base of the pyramid, or physical needs, are fairly well met by most business organizations in the United States.

Close on the heels of physical needs are safety needs. Employees want to feel safe—not stifled, safe. Safety needs include security, stability, protection, and freedom from fear (both physical and psychological), anxiety and chaos. This can be as simple as providing protection to employees going to and from the parking lot, or as complex as guaranteed job security, profit sharing, and the like.

Having demonstrated the effort to meet those needs, the employees now begin to feel they can trust the entrepreneur—and a prime objective of any entrepreneur is to develop a high-trust organization.

When employees feel that they are indeed an integral part of the corporate structure their need for belongingness will be met. It is human nature to desire a place in the group—in this case, the corporate family—and employees will strive mightily to attain that goal.

It is a wise entrepreneur who understands employees' need for belongingness, for without it, a feeling of detachment will prevail, preventing the organization from reaching its goals and objectives. Quite simply, when people feel they belong, they produce. As discussed in Chapter 6, when employees are working toward a common goal with shared values, they can and will help you realize your dreams.

In order to meet the needs of the employees, the entrepreneur must first affect a management and leadership style that allows for the encouragement of others. To do that, an entrepreneur must make the transition to Visionary Leader.

Remember that the four phases of entrepreneurial growth are:

Phase 1:   *Entrepreneurial Genius*
Phase 2:   *Benevolent Dictator*
Phase 3:   *Disassociated Director*
Phase 4:   *Visionary Leader*

When entrepreneurs find themselves facing the discomforts of Benevolent Dictator and Disassociated Director, they will often try to alleviate those discomforts by reverting to the more comfortable behavior of Entrepreneurial Genius. Unfortunately, doing so spells disaster for the organization. In business, as in life, you can never go back. Visionary Leadership is reached when the organization can be effectively led and managed without compromising the entrepreneur's greatest asset: Entrepreneurial Vision.

What is often missing in the earlier phases—Entrepreneurial Genius, Benevolent Dictator and Disassociated Director—is consistent, systematically planned communication, cooperation and collaboration.

Your transition to Visionary Leader will be made easier if you will remember two major points: One, you are working with adults, not children. If you are just starting out, treat your staff as the adults they are right from the beginning. If you have been in business a while, take an honest assessment of how you relate to your staff. If you find yourself treating them as children, stop and correct your behavior. The second point to remember is to know when it's time to relinquish control. Use your entrepreneurial skills and talents to attain high-leverage opportunities and let the organization's managers do their jobs.

When the entrepreneur's behavior is erratic, it is virtually impossible for the organization to become high-trust. And without trust, the organization will never reach its goals and objectives.

Understanding entrepreneurial behaviors, appreciating the motivations behind those behaviors, and modifying them can help shift Entrepreneurial Geniuses, Benevolent Dictators and Disassociated Directors into Visionary Leaders.

Visionary Leaders build companies that communicate, cooperate and collaborate. They share Values, Vision and Mission with the organization and its customers. They create purpose-driven organizations that achieve goals, meet objectives and provide satisfaction for employees, customers and vendors alike.

You have set yourself apart by reading this book. You have the dedication, commitment, and ability to put this information to use. I encourage you to share this book with your staff and management team. By working together, you have the power to impact and change the world. Use the tools presented throughout this book to become a Visionary Leader and make the Entrepreneurial Transition!

Make it so.

****

Index

Entrepreneurial Transitions
by Roy F. Cammarano

"Manage your organization for what you want it to become ... not for what it is and *never* for what it was."

(Please Print)   Date _____

Name _____

Company _____

Address _____

_____

City _____ State _____ Zip _____

Phone (_____) _____

Fax (_____) _____

Entrepreneurial Transitions
Roy F. Cammarano

PRICE	QTY.	AMOUNT
$16.95		
Sub-total		
For Delivery in Calif. Add 7.75% Sales Tax		
Shipping & Handling: 1st Book $2.00, Add'l Books $1.00 ea.		
TOTAL		

Payment Method

____ Check or money order (in U.S. funds) enclosed. Please make payable to:

Entrepreneurial Products, Inc.

____ Charge to VISA

____ Charge to MasterCard

Card Number _____

Expiration Date _____

Cardholder's Signature _____

Please return to:
Entrepreneurial Products, Inc.
34545 Scenic Drive
Dana Point, California 92629